"Stock car racing has got distinct possibilities for Sunday shows and we do not know how big it can be if it's handled properly. . . . It can go the same way as big car racing (Indianapolis). I believe stock car racing can become a nationally recognized sport by having a National Point Standing. . . . Stock car racing as we've been running it is not, in my opinion, the answer. . . . We must try to get track owners and promoters interested in building stock car racing up. We are all interested in one thing—that is, improving the present conditions. The answer lies in our group right here today to do it."

—Bill France Sr.

On December 14, 1947, speaking at NASCAR's organizational meeting at the Streamline Hotel in Daytona Beach, Florida, Bill France Sr. expressed his vision for stock car racing's future. A half-century later, France's words seem prophetic.

1948 ★ 1998

50 NASCAR

THE THUNDER OF AMERICA

HarperHorizon

an imprint of HarperCollins*Publishers*

A TEHABI BOOK

Tehabi Books, who designed and produced *NASCAR: The Thunder of America* has conceived and produced many award-winning, visually oriented books. "Tehabi," which symbolizes the spirit of teamwork, derives its name from the Hopi Indian tribe of the southwestern United States. Tehabi Books is located in Del Mar, California.

Chris Capen—*President;* Tom Lewis—*Editorial and Design Director;* Sharon Lewis—*Controller;*
Andy Lewis—*Art Director;* Nancy Cash—*Managing Editor;* Sam Lewis—*Webmaster;*
Ross Eberman—*Director of Corporate Sales;* Tim Connolly—*Sales and Marketing Manager;*
Bill Center—*Editor;* Sarah Morgans—*Copy Editor;* Gail Fink—*Copy Proofer.*
Additional support for NASCAR was provided by Bob Moore, Jim McLaurin, Bob Zellar, and Steve Waid.

www.tehabi.com

NASCAR: The Thunder of America was published by HarperHorizon,
an Imprint of HarperCollins Publishers, Inc., 10 East 53rd Street, New York, NY 10022.
John Silbersack—*Senior Vice President and Publishing Director;*
Ken Fund—*Senior Vice President Finance and Operations;*
Frank Fochetta—*Vice President and Director of HarperCollins Enterprises;*
Patricia Teberg—*Director of Brand Publishing;* Amy Wasserman—*Marketing Director.*

www.harpercollins.com

With special thanks to key individuals at NASCAR for their contributions
in the creation of *NASCAR: The Thunder of America.*
Paul Brooks—*Director of Special Projects and Publishing;* Kelly Crouch—*Editorial Manager;*
Kevin Triplett—*Director of Operations;* Erica Negedly—*Secretary to Kevin Triplett;*
Bob Mauk—*Former Assistant to William H. G. France;* Jonathan V. Mauk—*Director of Archives.*

www.nascar.com

Library of Congress Cataloging-in-Publication Data
NASCAR: the thunder of America
p.   cm.
ISBN: 0-06-105060-1 (hardcover). — ISBN: 0-06-105075-X (leatherbound).
1. Stock car racing—United States—History.
2. Stock car racing—United States—History—Pictoral works.
3. NASCAR (Association)—History. I. NASCAR (Association)
GV1029.9.S74N377 1998
796.72'0973--dc21   97-50245
CIP

98 99 00 01 02 / TB 10 9 8 7 6 5 4 3 2 1

This edition is printed on acid-free paper that meets the American National Standards Institute Z39.48 Standard.
Printed in Korea through Dai Nippon Printing Co., Ltd.

GOOD**Y**YEAR

**t
a
b
l
e**

**o
f**

**c
o
n
t
e
n
t
s**

The Thunder of America
page 18

Competition
page 34

Triumph
page 66

Devotion
page 90

Family
page 116

Teamwork
page 140

Spirit
page 170

The events of a NASCAR Winston Cup weekend are reflected in the helmet of Rusty Wallace, the 1989 NASCAR Winston Cup Series champion.

"An edge used to last for two or three races. Now it can come and go during a closer than they ever have before." —Seven-time NASCAR Winston Cup Series champion Dale Earnhardt

COMPETITION

race. From top to bottom, everyone works harder and runs faster and

The pack runs door-to-door as well as bumper-to-bumper at Charlotte, North Carolina, in May 1997.

"Winning is reaching the top of the mountain. And winning

Paul Goldsmith scored a victory of historic significance in 1958 when he won the final stock car race on Daytona's old Beach-Road course.

TRIUMPH

"one of the **majors** is standing on top of the world."

—Cale Yarborough, the only driver to win five Southern 500s at Darlington

"To look out on the infield on Sunday morning, to see the the teams when the National Anthem is being played. It my heart skips a beat. Always has, always will."

DEVOTION

flags and the people, and to look down on the cars and gives me shivers every time. When the engines start,

—NASCAR fan Nanci Allen-White, Cincinnati, Ohio

Banners fly over the infield at Michigan International Speedway on June 23, 1996.

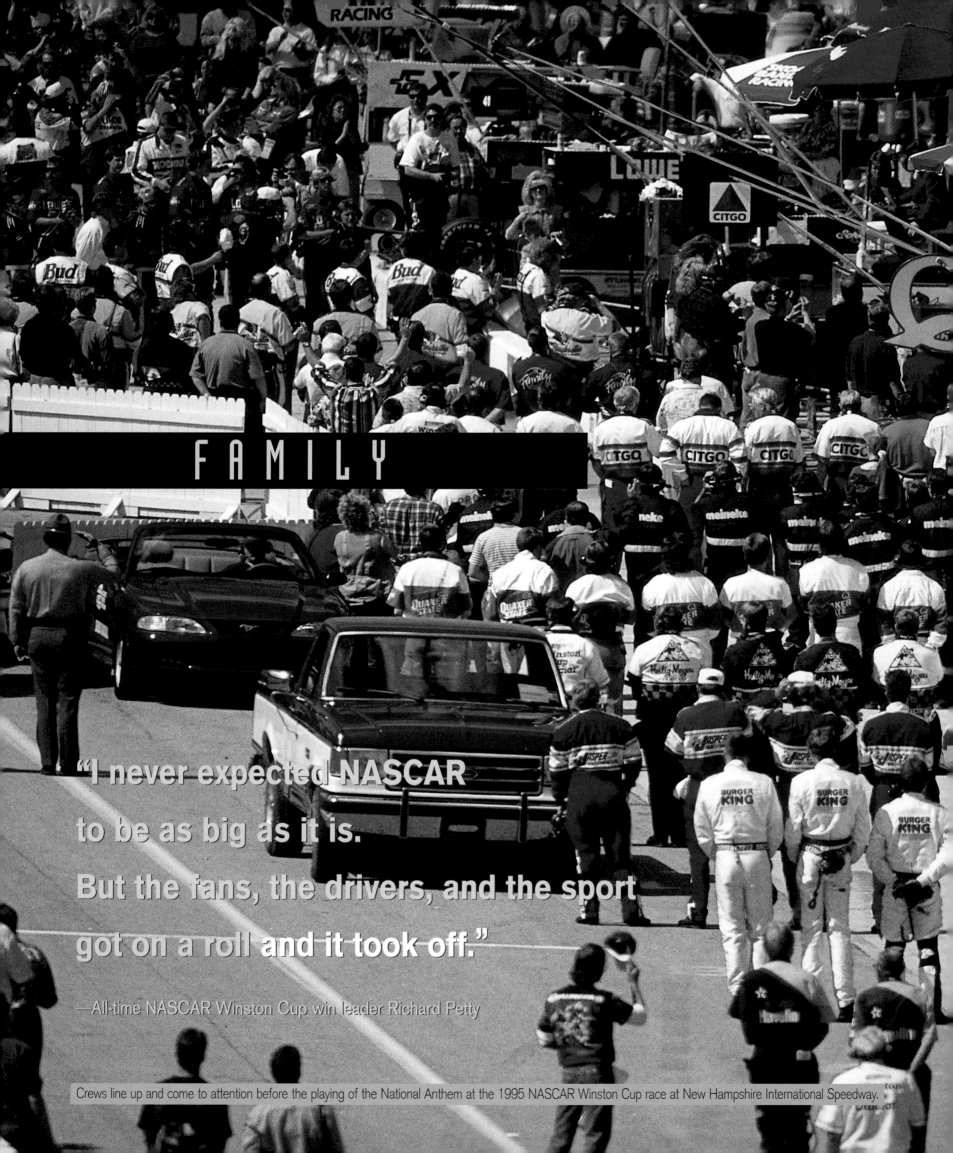

FAMILY

"I never expected NASCAR
to be as big as it is.
But the fans, the drivers, and the sport
got on a roll **and it took off.**"

—All-time NASCAR Winston Cup win leader Richard Petty

Crews line up and come to attention before the playing of the National Anthem at the 1995 NASCAR Winston Cup race at New Hampshire International Speedway.

"Teamwork is everything. It takes all of us working together.

—Two-time NASCAR Winston Cup Series champion Jeff Gordon on the importance of his "Rainbow Warriors" crew

TEAMWORK

Despite the efforts of his crew during this pit stop, Gordon finished second to Dale Jarrett at Pocono, Pennsylvania, in July 1997.

S P I R I T

"I went out one night in the '40s and watched what was going on. and went racing. I came along too soon to be a part of how big it the sport. I love racing." —Herb Thomas, first two-time NASCAR Grand National champion

I figured if they could do it, so could I. So I went home, built a car,

has become. But I wouldn't give nothin' in the world for my time in

"It is so hard to move up on the track.

You can have a great car but be stuck in 15th because the guy in front of you is just as strong.

He's fighting the same battle . . . and it's the same thing all the way up to the leader.

The competition is that intense.

If you have a bad pit stop or if the driver messes up and you lose three or four spots,

you have a tough time getting them back."

—1995 NASCAR Craftsman Truck Series champion Mike Skinner, who is now racing in the NASCAR Winston Cup Series

Mike Skinner (car No. 31) runs ahead of Kyle Petty in traffic during the March 9, 1997, race at Atlanta Motor Speedway.

Screaming 700-horsepower engines. High-banked ovals. The exotic aroma of rubber and fuel. A brilliant rainbow of cars blurring into the turns. The precision of choreographed pit crews. The roar of hundreds of thousands of fans.

In the last fifty years, America has seen the emergence of a culture that embraces a competition built around powerful machines and steel-willed men.

Fifty years of dogged determination, tactical planning, state-of-the-art technology, and seat-of-the-pants tinkering.

Fifty years of an astounding work ethic.

Fifty years punctuated by the incredible efforts of Richard Petty and Dale Earnhardt; "Fireball" Roberts and Joe Weatherly; Bud Moore, Junie Donlavey, and the Wood Brothers; the Labontes and the Allisons; the legends of yesteryear and those emerging "Young Guns" of NASCAR's future.

Week after week, month after month spent pursuing the grueling NASCAR racing seasons simply to be a single car length—or less—faster than anyone else, whether after five hundred miles of the Daytona 500 or fifty laps of wheel-to-wheel combat in weekly Saturday night shows around the country.

"Stock car racing is as American as you can get," Junior Johnson once observed. "You've got both tradition and excitement. It's men and machines in competition together. As a country, we grew up building better stuff. As a sport, stock car racing shows what that country can do."

Which might explain why NASCAR racing is America's fastest-growing sport, with a 50th anniversary that attests to its lasting appeal.

The threads of American values are woven throughout NASCAR. Competition. Triumph. Devotion. Family. Teamwork. Spirit. It's all in NASCAR.

"Why are we successful?" Darrell Waltrip asked rhetorically. "The more people see us, the more they like us. Why? Because we're pretty much them. Fans can relate to us. We're driving cars. Everyone drives cars."

NASCAR racers drive cars with a passion that reaches into the souls of their fans. The drivers are an extension of the American dream to go fast, be exciting, and leave a mark.

"I think the 'I can do that' aspect of the sport cannot be minimized," said Waltrip's brother Michael while matching wits with fans at a racing simulator. "The fans here today know they can't be on the track. But if they beat my time here on the simulator, they've got something to take home."

Putting the fans as close to the driver's seat—and the drivers—as possible is a key to NASCAR's success. NASCAR sees the fans as an integral part of the family that Bill France started building in 1948 when his National Association for Stock Car Auto Racing began sanctioning races.

To this day, NASCAR remains an organization run by the France family—the sport taking precedence over the needs and desires of any individual.

The feeling of family extends throughout the sport. Brothers work with brothers, fathers with sons. Bill France Sr. with Bill Jr. and Jim . . . and the sons with their heirs. The Pettys, Allisons, Woods, Labontes, Waltrips, Bodines, Elliotts, and countless small family teams working out of tiny garages across the land. All part of the family. All practicing the same teamwork that ultimately results in lightning-fast pit stops at the NASCAR Winston Cup level.

And the goal of that teamwork is to compete as much as to triumph. Yes, the sport has great champions. But it has far more competitors devoted to the idea of racing than concerned with winning track championships or national titles.

For fifty years, the NASCAR family has included weekend hobbyists as well as career professional drivers. NASCAR has a rich tradition.

Yet NASCAR racing is still young enough that it is literally in the midst of reshaping itself into a major national sport with a schedule that is being transformed to include races in many of the big metropolitan areas around the country.

Fifty years of NASCAR racing. Half a century. Still, a span of time short enough that some of today's greatest stars actually raced with the founding drivers of NASCAR. The bridge from then to now is still intact. Buck Baker, who finished 11th in the first NASCAR Strictly Stock race at Charlotte, North Carolina, in 1949, was still behind the wheel at Daytona in the 1976 Firecracker 400. In that same race, a painfully shy Georgia country boy named Bill Elliott finished 19th. Baker finished his career that year, and Elliott began his.

NASCAR has deep roots planted firmly in the stock cars competing every Saturday night on the dirt bullrings and short asphalt ovals across the land. There are more than 130 tracks in the NASCAR family that host 2,200 events annually. On even the smallest of tracks, many drivers pursue the dream of racing onward and upward into the NASCAR Craftsman Truck Series; NASCAR Busch Series, Grand National Division; and ultimately competing on the ultramodern superspeedways of the NASCAR Winston Cup Series.

NASCAR has grown to fill the need for a fast-paced America that thrives on excitement and close competition. And we don't mind it loud either. On the brink of the 21st century, we like it loud and raucous, breathtaking and thrilling.

America sees the competitiveness and astounding work ethic of this sport. America has seen it . . . and fallen in love with NASCAR.

**"I had to decide whether to retire from automobile racing
and get a motel or something, or to put everything we had into the track.
We've put everything we've made back into motorsports,
and I don't think I'll ever get tired of it."**

—Bill France Sr.

In the early days, France, shown promoting the 1950 Speedweeks at Daytona Beach, Florida, was both NASCAR's president and marketing man.

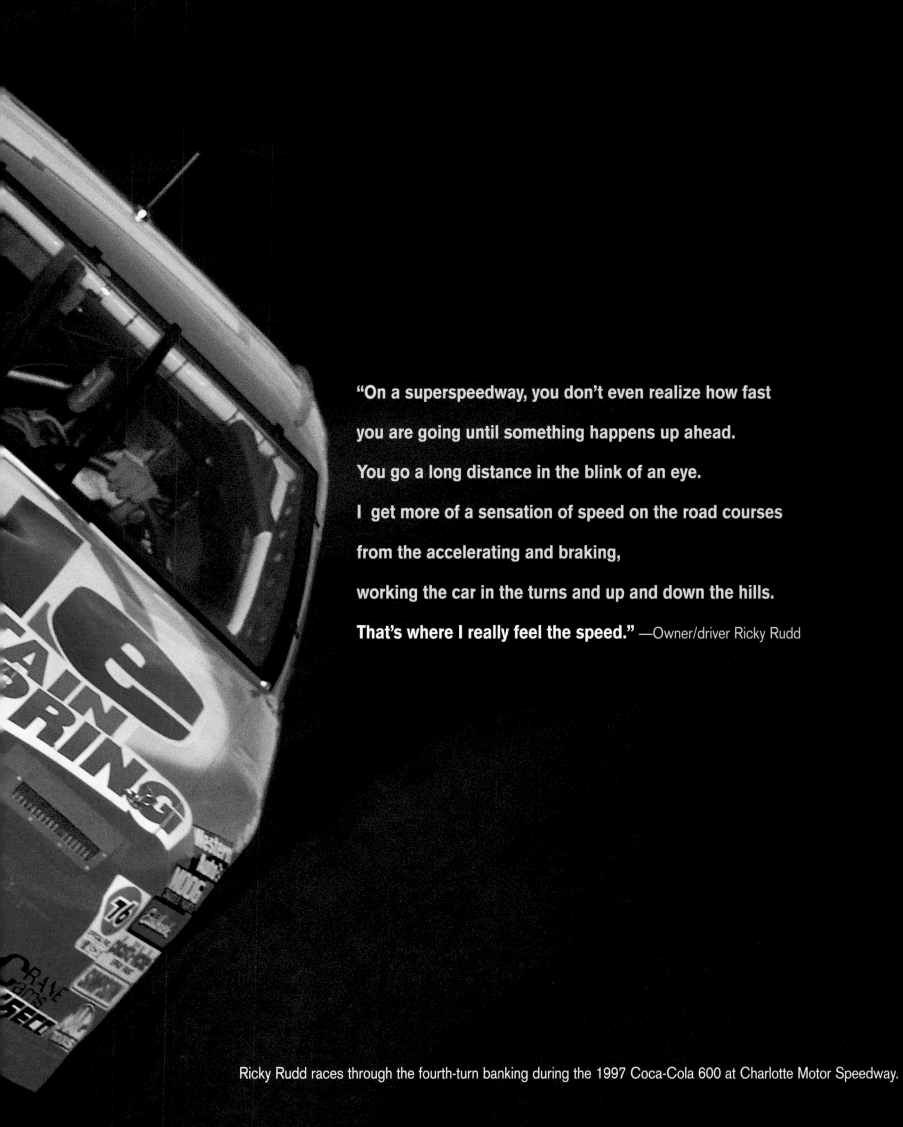

"On a superspeedway, you don't even realize how fast

you are going until something happens up ahead.

You go a long distance in the blink of an eye.

I get more of a sensation of speed on the road courses

from the accelerating and braking,

working the car in the turns and up and down the hills.

That's where I really feel the speed." —Owner/driver Ricky Rudd

Ricky Rudd races through the fourth-turn banking during the 1997 Coca-Cola 600 at Charlotte Motor Speedway.

"The grandstands come alive under your feet.

I don't know if it is the cars or the people who create that feeling.

But it's a great sensation. Every time the pack comes around, the grandstands come alive.

You can hear and feel it. It's exciting and exhausting."

—NASCAR fan Greg Drummer of Dallas, Texas

The grandstands at Daytona International Speedway are packed for the 1996 Daytona 500.

Ralph Earnhardt won hundreds of career short track races and the NASCAR Late Model Sportsman title in 1956.

Ray Hendrick ranks among NASCAR's all-time great short-track drivers with more than 500 wins in Modified and Late Model Sportsman Divisions.

Fred Lorenzen was the first NASCAR driver to win more than $100,000 in a season and won twenty-six NASCAR Winston Cup races.

Jack Ingram (left) won three straight NASCAR Late Model Sportsman Division championships (1972–74) and two NASCAR Busch Series titles (1982 and 1985).

Cotton Owens won more than 400 Modified and Late Model Sportsman races before becoming a successful car owner in the 1960s.

A. J. Foyt broke from his IndyCar schedule to win seven NASCAR Winston Cup races, including the 1972 Daytona 500.

Bob Welborn won twenty races and three straight NASCAR Convertible Division titles from 1955-1957 as well as seven NASCAR Winston Cup races in his career.

LeeRoy Yarbrough swept the Daytona 500, World 600, and Southern 500 in 1969 before there was a $1 million bonus for the feat.

Marshall Teague was a pioneer who posted seven NASCAR Winston Cup wins as he battled for early NASCAR driving supremacy.

Benny Parsons launched his NASCAR Winston Cup career after driving taxis in Detroit and won twenty-one races and the 1973 title.

Marvin Panch, the 1961 winner of the Daytona 500, won seventeen career NASCAR Winston Cup races, including eight from 1963-1965 for the Wood Brothers.

Red Farmer won three straight NASCAR Late Model Sportsman Division titles (1969–71) plus 1956 NASCAR Modified Division.

Glen Wood won hundreds of short-track races before capturing four NASCAR Winston Cup wins and then joining brother Leonard to win ninety-two races as owners.

Bobby Isaac, the 1970 NASCAR Winston Cup champion, earned thirty-seven wins and fifty-one poles at NASCAR's top level.

Jerry Cook won six NASCAR Modified Division championships in a seven-year span (1971–72, 1974–77).

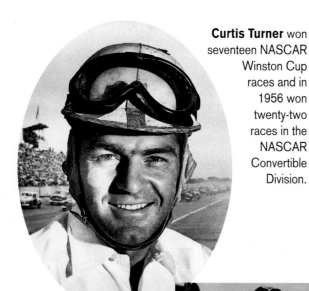

Curtis Turner won seventeen NASCAR Winston Cup races and in 1956 won twenty-two races in the NASCAR Convertible Division.

Lee Petty was the first three-time winner of the NASCAR Winston Cup Series season championship.

Glenn "Fireball" Roberts had four wins and five poles in the first ten races at Daytona International Speedway.

Herb Thomas won forty-nine NASCAR Winston Cup races and was the first driver to win two season championships (1951 and 1953).

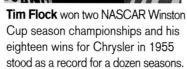

Tim Flock won two NASCAR Winston Cup season championships and his eighteen wins for Chrysler in 1955 stood as a record for a dozen seasons.

Red Byron won championships in NASCAR's first two seasons—in Modifieds in 1948 and NASCAR Winston Cup in 1949.

Junior Johnson won fifty NASCAR Winston Cup races as a driver and six NASCAR Winston Cup titles as an owner.

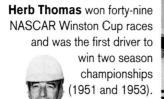

Joe Weatherly, the 1953 NASCAR Modified Division champ, won the NASCAR Winston Cup title in 1962 and 1963.

Buck Baker won forty-six NASCAR Winston Cup races and was the first driver to win back-to-back series championships (1956–57).

Rex White won twenty-six races and the 1960 championship during his NASCAR Winston Cup career.

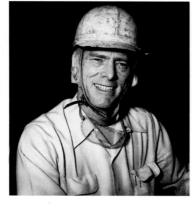

Fifty years. Fifty great drivers.
The cream of the crop of America's best NASCAR racers.
From the dirt ovals that hosted NASCAR's first Modified races in 1948 to the purely American modern superspeedways, from those boxy post–World War II sedans to the aerodynamically designed cars of today, one thing remains unchanged in NASCAR racing–the men behind the wheel.

THE FIFTY GREATEST NASCAR DRIVERS

The line of champions begins with Red Byron, NASCAR's first champion, and continues today with the Jeff Gordon generation of drivers. In between are race-tested winners like seventime NASCAR Winston Cup Series champions Richard Petty and Dale Earnhardt.

Twenty-two men have won at least one NASCAR Winston Cup Series season championship and thirteen have won more than one. But among the greatest drivers are those who have never won a NASCAR Winston Cup championship—men like "Fireball" Roberts, Junior Johnson, Curtis Turner, and Fred Lorenzen.

Selected by a panel of NASCAR experts, these fifty greatest drivers are not only from the NASCAR Winston Cup Series, but are the fifty greatest drivers from the spectrum of NASCAR racing.

There are Modified champions like Richie Evans, as well as division champions like Ralph Earnhardt, Jack Ingram, and Hershel McGriff. Drivers who had long and distinguished careers are counted in this reckoning, as are those who shared their time racing in NASCAR with other endeavors and those who had shorter but brilliant careers. Some whose careers were ebbing when NASCAR began and some whose careers will extend well into the 21st century are accounted for here.

26

FORMATION OF NASCAR, 1947
Red Byron
Herb Thomas
Marshall Teague
Lee Petty
Tim Flock
Buck Baker
Glen Wood
Bob Welborn
Joe Weatherly
"Fireball" Roberts
Cotton Owens
Junior Johnson
Curtis Turner
Ralph Earnhardt
Ned Jarrett
Richard Petty
Fred Lorenzen
Rex White
Hershel McGriff
Marvin Panch
Bobby Isaac
David Pearson
Ray Hendrick
LeeRoy Yarbrough
Tiny Lund
Benny Parsons

We begin with those who were around at the beginning—drivers who challenged the limits with modifieds and stock cars in those formative years on dirt ovals and the earliest paved speedways.

Herb Thomas, the Flock brothers, Buck Baker, Joe Weatherly, and Lee Petty helped set the stage for the second generation that included the sons of Lee (Richard) and Buck (Buddy) plus drivers like David Pearson and Bobby Allison.

Today, NASCAR racing is America's fastest-growing sport. But in the green years when

THE FIFTY GREATEST NASCAR DRIVERS fans nationwide were just beginning to take notice, the impetus was supplied by "the King" Richard Petty and a court that included Pearson, Cale Yarborough, Bobby Isaac, and Darrell Waltrip. The torch was passed to another generation led by Dale Earnhardt and on again to the latest generation with Jeff Gordon riding point.

The common bond for the past half-century is NASCAR, a tight-knit organization that is devoted totally to the American sport of stock car racing.

NASCAR is more than a sanctioning body. It is a spirit that can be found on Saturday nights at local tracks across the land as well as high-banked superspeedways on Sunday afternoons.

NASCAR is the races of NASCAR Winston Racing Series as well as the NASCAR Winston Cup and the NASCAR Busch Series. It is modifieds and trucks as well as stock cars. NASCAR is the machines—and the men and women who design, build, service, and drive them.

Here are NASCAR's greats—it's past, present, and future expressed in the exploits and triumphs of fifty men. The fifty great drivers who have helped steer NASCAR to the forefront of the American sports scene.

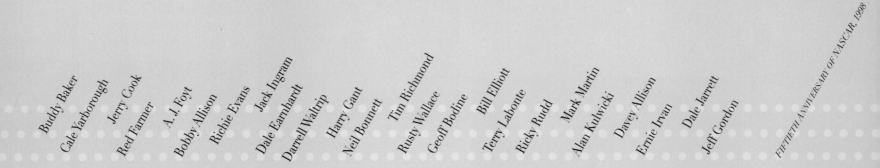

Buddy Baker Cale Yarborough Jerry Cook Red Farmer A. J. Foyt Bobby Allison Richie Evans Jack Ingram Dale Earnhardt Darrell Waltrip Harry Gant Neil Bonnett Tim Richmond Rusty Wallace Geoff Bodine Bill Elliott Terry Labonte Ricky Rudd Mark Martin Alan Kulwicki Davey Allison Ernie Irvan Dale Jarrett Jeff Gordon

FIFTIETH ANNIVERSARY OF NASCAR, 1998

1980s   1990s

Rusty Wallace, who has forty-seven NASCAR Winston Cup wins, won the 1989 season championship and twice finished second.

Neil Bonnett was a short-track star who, as a member of the Alabama Gang, won eighteen times during his NASCAR Winston Cup Career.

Geoff Bodine, like many before him, starred in the NASCAR Modified ranks before starting a NASCAR Winston Cup career in which he won eighteen times.

Mark Martin, the all-time winner on the NASCAR Busch Series tour, posted twenty-two wins in his stellar NASCAR Winston Cup career.

Terry Labonte has started more consecutive races than anyone in NASCAR Winston Cup history, winning two Series titles (1984 and 1996).

Jeff Gordon won twenty-seven races and two NASCAR Winston Cup Series championships between 1995–97.

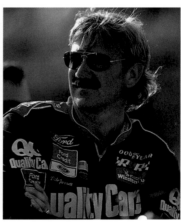

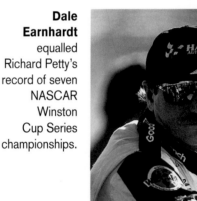

Dale Earnhardt equalled Richard Petty's record of seven NASCAR Winston Cup Series championships.

David Pearson ranks second in NASCAR Winston Cup wins (105) and poles (113). He also won three season titles.

Darrell Waltrip won eighty-four NASCAR Winston Cup races, including forty-three wins and three titles driving for Junior Johnson.

Dale Jarrett has won fifteen NASCAR Winston Cup races, including two Daytona 500s, and was series runner-up in 1997.

Bill Elliott, the 1988 NASCAR Winston Cup champ, has forty career wins, including eleven and the Winston Million in 1985.

Ernie Irvan won short-track titles on both the East and West Coasts before moving to a NASCAR Winston Cup career in which he captured fifteen wins.

Ricky Rudd won at least one NASCAR Winston Cup race a year for fifteen straight seasons, including four as an owner-driver.

Tiny Lund won four NASCAR Grand American crowns as well as the 1963 Daytona 500.

Davey Allison won in just his fourteenth career start and went on to win eighteen more times in his brief but brilliant NASCAR Winston Cup career.

Harry Gant (right) was the oldest driver to win a NASCAR Winston Cup race at fifty-two and once won four straight races.

Richie Evans won a record nine NASCAR Featherlite Modified Tour titles, including eight straight (1978–85).

Hershel McGriff has won NASCAR races in the last six decades and won the Mexican Road Race in 1950 with Bill France Sr.

Cale Yarborough won eighty-three races and is the only driver to win three straight NASCAR Winston Cup Series championships (1976–78).

Richard Petty won a record 200 NASCAR Winston Cup races en route to seven season titles.

Ned Jarrett won two season titles in both the NASCAR Winston Cup and Late Model Sportsman Divisions.

Tim Richmond came to the NASCAR Winston Cup Series after an IndyCar career and won thirteen races.

Alan Kulwicki won five career NASCAR Winston Cup races as well as the 1992 series title by just ten points, the closest margin in history.

Bobby Allison, the 1964 and 1965 NASCAR Modified champ, won eighty-four NASCAR Winston Cup races and the 1983 series championship.

Buddy Baker, the first driver to officially break the 200 mph mark, earned nineteen career NASCAR Winston Cup wins.

"**Speed, . . . thrills, excitement,** and the love for the drivers and the fans. Nothing can compare to the greatest sport in the world—NASCAR."

—NASCAR fan Carl Cummings, Chesapeake, Virginia

Former NASCAR Winston Cup champion Terry Labonte (car No. 5) races past Ernie Irvan (car No. 28) and Ted Musgrave (car No. 16).

COMPETITION

"Trucks have

their own characteristics.

They're not very aerodynamic,

but they are rocketships.

They are as much fun

as anything I've driven."

—1997 NASCAR Craftsman Truck Series

champion Jack Sprague

Jack Sprague races toward the NASCAR

Craftsman Truck Series championship at the Phoenix

International Raceway on November 1, 1997. Sprague

began his NASCAR career in the NASCAR Winston

Racing Series on short tracks in Michigan. He has also

raced in the NASCAR Busch Series and the

NASCAR Winston Cup Series.

Take away the glitz and glamour, get the big-budget sponsors' logos off the cars—even remove the fans—and you'll still have the heart of NASCAR racing: the competition.

Good competition is the glue that holds the sport together and always will be. Indeed, NASCAR's roots were planted by a couple of guys trying to settle bets over whose car was faster. They did so, competing head-to-head on backroads and in

IT'S ABOUT COMPETITION open fields.

That basic principle was never lost on Harry Gant, who remembers his early years racing on small ovals as fondly as those spent under the spotlight of the NASCAR Winston Cup Series.

"We traveled with about four different cars," Gant recalls. "Every night, it'd be a different track. We'd go in and take on each track's best drivers. Every place we'd visit, it'd be big news in town. Then we'd drive overnight to the next track, and it'd be big news all over again."

The places weren't superspeedways. Some were no bigger than a parking lot. Some weren't paved. But the lure was the foundation of the sport—competition.

The drive to be the best. Without competition, there would be no sport.

Those who disagree need look no further than Gant or present NASCAR Winston Cup star Ken Schrader.

Despite his success on the premier level of the sport, Schrader continues to load up his schedule with driving stints in various divisions on both superspeedways and local short tracks around the country. It's not unusual to see Schrader—as Gant and Bobby Allison once did—race in a NASCAR Winston Cup event on Sunday, then make a stop at a local track during the week.

"I guess the most races we've run in a year has been ninety-four," Schrader says. "I like doing about eighty a year. On off-weekends I still want to run some stuff, or do some midweek races during the summer."

For the Schraders, Allisons, and Gants of the sport, it's not about money; it's all about competition.

They are not alone. That same competitive nature is behind virtually everyone racing in any of NASCAR's twelve touring divisions as well as those racing at the small, lesser known bullrings around the country.

Clearly, money isn't the reason they're racing at the grassroots level. Costs notwithstanding, drivers are there for the battle.

Man against man. Machine against machine. Putting everything on the line to prove who has the fastest car.

It's the drive, the inner desire to win, that is the common thread running between those who race banged-up street stocks on Saturday nights and the superstars of NASCAR Winston Cup racing. And whether the race is held on a flat three-eighths-mile track in California or the high-banked superspeedway at Talladega, Alabama, the stakes are the same: winning or losing.

Under NASCAR's watchful eye, close competition is the ultimate goal. To keep the teams equal in performance,

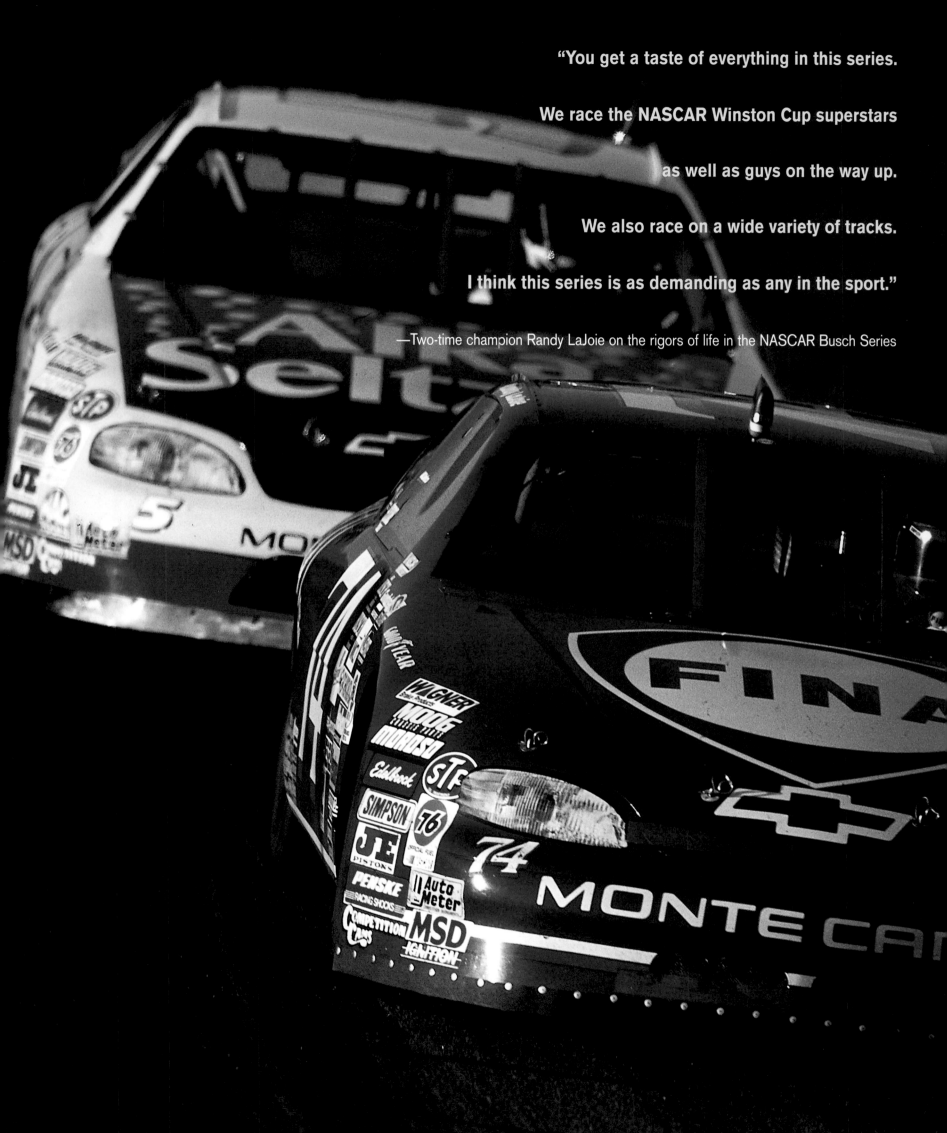

"You get a taste of everything in this series.

We race the NASCAR Winston Cup superstars

as well as guys on the way up.

We also race on a wide variety of tracks.

I think this series is as demanding as any in the sport."

—Two-time champion Randy LaJoie on the rigors of life in the NASCAR Busch Series

NASCAR limits big-buck technological advances that could make one team stand head and fenders above the rest. While costs are a factor, too, NASCAR wants nothing more than to have every car that starts each race heading for the checkered flag on the final lap.

It works. With the current level of intense competition, qualifying has become as important as, if not more critical than, the race itself. The difference in speeds between the polesitter and the last qualifier is often marked in barely measurable slivers of a second. And it's not uncommon to see big-name drivers go home, unable to make the starting field.

Close competition is a basic tenet to all of NASCAR's divisions, especially to the NASCAR Busch Series and the NASCAR Craftsman Truck Series.

"The birth of the NASCAR Craftsman Truck Series has created a demand for more people," Schrader said. "And there are drivers, crew chiefs, and crewmen at smaller short tracks around the country who, with a little bit of guidance, could be ready to go within a couple of years."

Some are already there.

Just scan the NASCAR Winston Cup roster and you'll find names that have come directly from any one or more of NASCAR's tough divisions. Geoff and Brett Bodine, Greg Sacks, Jimmy Spencer, and Steve Park all honed their skills in NASCAR's Featherlite Modified Tour. Ricky Craven broke in through the NASCAR Busch and Busch North Series. Folks such as Johnny Benson, Jeff Gordon, and Dale Jarrett came through the NASCAR Busch Series. And Kenny Irwin Jr. and Mike Skinner can thank the NASCAR Craftsman Truck Series for their shot at the big time.

They'll soon be joined by others who have taken the same path. Among the ranks of NASCAR's touring series participants are countless others who are working their way up the ladder—facing tougher competition at each step toward the NASCAR Winston Cup Series.

Sure, along with every advancement come higher stakes and greater financial reward. But ask any of those drivers what they would do if they had to make the choice between money and winning a championship trophy. No surprise, they'd all choose the trophy over the cash.

Perhaps Mark Martin summed it up best while in the thick of another championship battle, with literally millions in prize money and endorsements at stake.

"This is all about competition," he said. "And I'm just glad to be competing and to be a contender."

—Richard Huff

"On a short track, comparing a regular stock car and a modified

is like chasing a school bus with a Ferrari.

We're NASCAR's oldest division and I think the most exciting.

We're the best-handling, quickest-turning short-track cars NASCAR has.

I get more thrills from driving a modified than anything else." —Mike Stefanik

Stefanik, of Coventry, Rhode Island, scored a rare double in 1997 when he won both the NASCAR Featherlite Modified

Tour championship (for the third time) and the NASCAR Busch North Series title.

Stefanik became the first driver to win two NASCAR series in the same year since Lee Petty in 1958.

"It's tough to win in any **NASCAR** division. The guys on local tracks

are just as competitive as the guys in the **NASCAR** Winston Cup cars."

—Ron Hornaday Jr., who won two NASCAR Featherlite Southwest Tour titles

before winning the 1995 NASCAR Craftsman Truck Series championship

Joe Ruttman (truck No. 80) and Rich Bickle (truck No. 17) battle during the NASCAR Craftsman Truck race at Martinsville Speedway on September 27, 1997.

"My career is mostly in short-track racing. I just have a knack for getting through traffic when I start in the back. The advantage I have is I can race ahead of myself, looking a lap or two ahead and setting up the cars I have to pass."

—Larry Phillips, five-time NASCAR Winston Racing Series national champion

The NASCAR racing program includes twelve touring series, ranging from the weekly NASCAR Winston Racing Series events held on local short tracks across the country, all the way up to the prestigious NASCAR Winston Cup Series. Cajon Speedway, in El Cajon, California, top, runs the NASCAR Winston Racing Series, while other tracks like Lanier Raceway, in Gainesville, Georgia, above, run the NASCAR Slim Jim All Pro Series.

Dale Earnhardt, "the Intimidator," goes low to make a three-wide pass on Jeff Burton and Dave Marcis.

"Dale Earnhardt is the consummate professional athlete. He is dedicated, focused, smart, and in excellent physical condition. And he's a determined competitor who refuses to lose . . . and absolutely refuses to give up. Dale is the yardstick. He's been the best for a long time."

—NASCAR Winston Cup driver
Darrell Waltrip

44

"It's still awe-inspiring when I look down pit lane during a round of stops. It looks chaotic, but it's precision choreography. Six men on forty different cars, all racing the clock against an assigned task. The degree of perfection is incredibly high when you consider everything that can go wrong. It used to be that you could gain ground with a good pit stop. Now you lose a lot of ground if you make the slightest mistake."

—Car owner Robert Yates

Working stop watches with both hands while communicating over his headset radio, car owner Robert Yates, below, tracks the progress of drivers Dale Jarrett and Ernie Irvan during a NASCAR Winston Cup race.

The action is fast and furious as the entire field pits during a caution period.

"That was wild . . . absolutely wild."

—David Pearson after winning the 1976 Daytona 500 despite a last-turn collision with Richard Petty

Pearson coaxed his heavily damaged Mercury to the checkered flag and the awards ceremony.

There they were on live television, the icons of NASCAR racing, Richard Petty and David Pearson, caught in one of those moments that define a sport.

With baseball, it was Bobby Thomson's homer in 1951. With football, it was Baltimore's overtime victory against the New York Giants in the 1958 championship game. In NASCAR, it was the 1976 Daytona 500 when America stood up and took notice . . . thanks to Petty, Pearson, and the cameras of ABC.

The network decided to experiment in 1976 and show the finish of NASCAR's premier event live nationally. What the cameras caught fueled the imagination of a nation. Entering the final turn of the last lap, Petty drove low on the track in desperate pursuit of race leader Pearson. For a split second, the NASCAR Winston Cup's all-time winningest drivers—"the King" and "the Silver Fox"—were side by side. Then they touched. And they spun. Petty crashed hard into the outside wall. Pearson's heavily damaged car slid down onto the apron between the track and pit lane. Somehow, Pearson managed to keep the engine running and chugged ever so slowly to the checkered flag as Petty's car smoked in the background.

Great drama. Great finish. Great television.

And if that race whetted the nation's appetite for NASCAR, another Daytona 500 three years later secured both the future of the sport and its place on television. In 1979, CBS gambled with the first live "flag-to-flag" coverage of a stock car race. This time, NASCAR provided drama worthy of an Emmy-winning miniseries. After bumping one another down the length of the backstretch in a duel for the lead, Cale Yarborough and Donnie Allison crashed while entering the third turn of the last lap. As Yarborough and Allison slid off into the infield, Petty raced around to a stunning victory. But it wasn't over. Back at the crash site, Yarborough was engaged in a brief but heavily publicized fistfight with Bobby Allison, who had parked at the scene to lend his brother support.

Timing is everything. So, too, in this age, is television. But tradition also plays a major role in selecting NASCAR's greatest races. It began with NASCAR's first finish ever on February 15, 1948, on the Beach-Road course at Daytona Beach, Florida. Red Byron, who would later become NASCAR's first season champion, won.

Sixteen months later, on a washboard dirt track off Wilkinson Boulevard in Charlotte, North Carolina, thirty-three drivers fought through dust and each other to complete 200 laps (150 miles) of the first NASCAR Strictly Stock Series race—later known as the NASCAR Grand National Series and still later as the NASCAR Winston Cup Series. Before a throng of somewhat startled spectators, Glenn Dunnaway won, but was disqualified for having "altered rear springs." Jim Roper, who had learned of the race while perusing a "Smilin' Jack" comic strip back in Great Bend, Kansas, was declared the winner in a hot rod Lincoln he had driven to the race.

The first superspeedway opened the following year. Named Darlington Raceway, the oblong oval sculpted from South Carolina farmland was NASCAR racing's answer to Indianapolis. The first Southern 500 was also NASCAR's first 500-mile race.

Seventy-five cars started. They raced for 6 hours, 38 minutes, and 40 seconds. In the end, Johnny Mantz won, thanks to better tires and experience on other paved tracks.

At the start of NASCAR's second decade came the long-anticipated opening of Daytona International Speedway, a stunning design for high-speed racing and a replacement for the old Beach-Road course on the Atlantic Ocean. The first Daytona 500 on February 22, 1959, produced a finish so close that officials needed three days to name a winner. Three cars—those of Lee Petty, Johnny Beauchamp, and the lapped Joe Weatherly—crossed the finish line side by side. A long study of photographs was needed to give Petty the victory in NASCAR's biggest event to that time.

A year later, Charlotte Motor Speedway opened and established a new standard—a 600-mile race. Joe Lee Johnson won the first World 600 on a long day that underlined the idea that endurance was as important as speed in the NASCAR vocabulary.

Daytona, Darlington, Charlotte, and Talladega produced great finishes as well as major events. Darlington hosted a riveting duel in the spring of 1979 as two eras crossed. Richard Petty and Darrell Waltrip swapped the lead several times over the tense closing laps of the Rebel 500 before Waltrip won by half a car length.

From left, the 1995 NASCAR Busch Series race at Rockingham finished a spectacular three cars wide with Todd Bodine (right) beating Mike Wallace (center) by six inches with Johnny Benson (left) another fraction of a second behind; the 1984 Winston 500 at Talladega Superspeedway produced a record seventy-five lead changes; the finish of the inaugural Daytona 500 was so close that it took three days to declare Lee Petty (car No. 42) the winner over Johnny Beauchamp (car No. 73).

Waltrip was in the hot seat again the following season in the World 600 at Charlotte, battling Benny Parsons for supremacy in NASCAR's longest race. They traded the lead eight times in the final twenty-six laps, with Parsons winning by five feet.

Talladega Superspeedway, opened in northern Alabama in 1969 with the promise of startling speeds and tight competition, and made good on that promise—perhaps no more so than in the 1981 Talladega 500. Raw rookie Ron Bouchard surprised Terry Labonte and Darrell Waltrip by leaving the last turn and outrunning them by inches in a 200-mph drag race to score his first and only NASCAR Winston Cup victory. At the same sprawling track in 1984, the NASCAR Winston 500 celebrated a landmark—a remarkable seventy-five lead changes ending in a Cale Yarborough victory.

"Winning might not be the only thing," Alan Kulwicki said after winning the NASCAR Winston Cup Series championship in 1992. "But it is the ultimate experience."

—*Mike Hembree*

"The best finish ever at Martinsville was that Dogwood Classic Modified race in 1981.

Richie Evans and Geoff Bodine got together off turn four going for the checkered flag.

Richie's car climbed the retaining wall so high

that you could read the roof number from the infield. But he never let off.

He bounced off the wall and bounced across the finish line

on three wheels for the win."

—Martinsville Speedway founder and CEO H. Clay Earles

Richie Evans accepts the winner's trophy after his wild Modified ride at Martinsville in 1981.

"If you can't be fast, be spectacular. Sometimes you're just an innocent and hope you're facing in the right direction when the car stops. Then you say a prayer

Musgrave rides the inside pit wall at Martinsville Speedway after a brush with Robert Pressley.

victim. All you can do when something goes wrong is to try to keep the engine running that the damage is not terminal." —Veteran NASCAR Winston Cup driver Ted Musgrave

"I think at some time that it's every little boy's dream to drive a race car.

I know it was my dream. I used to watch all the great drivers and say,

'That's what I want to do.' "

—Jeff Gordon, who started racing quarter-midgets at age five and grew up to be

a NASCAR Winston Cup Series champion at the age of twenty-four

The dreams that Bill France Jr., above, had at the wheel of a race car in the 1950s are no different than those shared by a young fan today, opposite.

"It might not be a contact sport, but it's a stand-up-for-what's-right sport. ... front by backing down." —Jimmy Spencer, NASCAR Winston Cup driver

The tire marks from a rival's car on the side of Jimmy Spencer's Ford show how intimate NASCAR's door-to-door racing can be.

Because he doesn't back down from close encounters, Spencer has been dubbed "Mr. Excitement" by his peers and fans.

You can't be afraid to mix it up. You don't move to the

They were the leaders of the famed Alabama Gang: brothers Bobby and Donnie Allison.

"They are as good as they come," David Pearson said of the Allisons. "They can drive anything to the limit."

And they often did.

The Allisons are among the most successful brother combinations in NASCAR Winston Cup history. Bobby won eighty-four races and the 1983 season championship. Donnie won ten races despite seldom racing a full season.

It was their ability to race everything and anywhere that set the Allisons apart. Bobby and Donnie campaigned in NASCAR's Modified and Late Model Sportsman divisions before reaching the NASCAR Winston Cup Series.

Donnie's forte was the high-speed superspeedways, where he produced nine of his victories and fifteen poles. He was considered one of the sport's premier high-speed drivers. In 1970, Donnie was Rookie of the Year at the Indianapolis 500.

"Donnie was as smooth at full speed as anyone I've ever seen," said Bobby, who also raced in the Indy 500 in 1973 and 1975.

Of the Allisons, Bobby was best known for his versatility and his desire to race as often as possible—a trait that made him a popular ambassador for NASCAR just as the general public was taking notice of NASCAR racing. Days after coming off the high banks at Daytona, Charlotte, or Talladega, Bobby might show up at a short track in Southern California or Missouri.

Given the opportunity, he'd race anywhere. **THE ALLISONS**

"I remember I showed up for a race one night out west and was introduced on a radio show," said Bobby. "The interviewer said, 'What a coincidence, a guy named Bobby Allison won a stock car race yesterday in North Carolina.' And I said, 'That would be me.'"

That would be Bobby Allison—all over the map promoting NASCAR by doing what he did best—racing.

"Bobby was one of the fiercest competitors that the sport has ever seen," said longtime rival Richard Petty. "He was one of the greatest drivers in history. We had many a great battle."

Bobby's greatest moment came during the 1988 Daytona 500 as he dueled son Davey to the checkered flag. Bobby won and Davey was second in the race's only one-two father-son finish.

Alas, the Allisons paid a price. The racing careers of Bobby and Donnie were shortened by injuries. And Davey died in a tragic helicopter accident just as his career hit full stride.

"The Allisons gave this sport all they had," said rival Cale Yarborough.

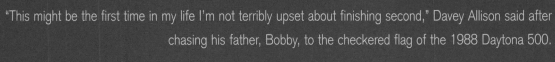
"This might be the first time in my life I'm not terribly upset about finishing second," Davey Allison said after chasing his father, Bobby, to the checkered flag of the 1988 Daytona 500.

Talladega Superspeedway has produced some of NASCAR's fastest, most exciting races.

Over its fifty years, NASCAR has raced just about everywhere—from Daytona's legendary Beach-Road course to the quarter-mile bullrings to the high-banked superspeedways to a Japanese road course.

And NASCAR has sanctioned just about every form of racing . . . including the Indy-type Speedway Division of the early '50s and the Drag Racing Division during the '60s, in addition to a variety of stock cars. The diversification has led to some unusual combinations.

The legendary Don Garlits ran his Swamp Rat I dragster down the backstretch of Daytona International Speedway at

SHORT TRACKS TO SUPERSPEEDWAYS

night. Other drag races and stock car races were held on the runways of abandoned World War II airbases and municipal airports.

The first race sanctioned by NASCAR, won by Red Byron in a Ford, was February 15, 1948, on the Beach-Road course—one mile down the two-lane strip of asphalt and a mile return across Daytona Beach's sand.

A year later, the Beach-Road course was expanded to 4.15 miles and the Daytona race became a dirt, asphalt, and drag race rolled into one with the Atlantic Ocean as a backdrop. Modifieds on the Beach-Road course hit speeds of 140 mph.

In the formative season, the short ovals were in vogue. Notable among the tracks was Bowman Gray Stadium at Winston-Salem, North Carolina—a quarter-mile, football stadium that's virtually unchanged to this day.

NASCAR's tracks come in all shapes and sizes besides the traditional oval.

Contrast Bowman Gray to the 2.66-mile, 33-degree banked tri-oval at Talladega Superspeedway in Alabama and the state-of-the-art tracks recently opened in Fontana, California; Fort Worth, Texas; Las Vegas, Nevada; and Homestead, Florida.

Road races date back to June 13, 1954, when NASCAR hosted an event on the runways of the airport at Linden, New Jersey. Al Keller won the race driving a Jaguar—the only time a foreign car has ever won a NASCAR race. A year later, a road race was run on the dirt course at Willow Springs Speedway in Lancaster, California—NASCAR's only race on a dirt road course.

Road America in Elkhart Lake, Wisconsin, began hosting NASCAR races on its 4.1-mile circuit in 1956. Southern California's Riverside Raceway was the lone road racing venue on the NASCAR Winston Cup tour for a number of seasons. Today, Riverside is gone but the road racing tradition lives on at Watkins Glen, New York, and Sears Point Raceway, north of San Francisco, California.

NASCAR has had triangles—from the two-mile track on the airbase at Montgomery, New York, used in 1960 to the present 2.5-mile circuit at

Slightly over a half-mile in length, the oval at Bristol, Tennessee, is a perfect arena for night races.

"The road course at Watkins Glen was always special

to my brothers and myself. To win here was a significant milestone in my career.

Leading through those turns and charging up the hill got to me."

—NASCAR Winston Cup driver Geoff Bodine

Bodine, a native New Yorker, fought off Bobby Labonte en route to victory at Watkins Glen in 1996.

Curtis Turner (car No. 26) slides coming out of a turn while in pursuit of Marvin Panch during a convertible race on the famed Daytona Beach-Road course on February 22, 1958.

"I think the races at Daytona will lose some of their glamour and interest

when they move the races away from the sand by the sea.

I wish the races could always be run on this spectacular course."

—Driver Mel Larson after NASCAR's last race on Daytona's Beach-Road course in 1958

Pocono, Pennsylvania. The one-mile track at Langhorne, Pennsylvania, was a perfect circle with the added obstacle of an underground spring that frequently used to wash out the first turn.

Dayton Speedway in Ohio started out as a squared dirt oval but was reconfigured with high banks for its first NASCAR Grand National race in 1950. It was there that Jimmy Florian gave Ford its first NASCAR Grand National victory.

The oval at North Wilkesboro, North Carolina, required drivers to race uphill on the backstretch and downhill on the front. North Wilkesboro was one of NASCAR's original tracks, hosting its first race on April 25, 1948, where as two years later, NASCAR's first superspeedway opened in Darlington, South Carolina—the 1.366-mile oval is egg shaped because the owner of the land didn't want his minnow pond outside turn two disturbed. The original pits at Darlington were on the apron of the racing surface and unprotected from race cars.

Among the strangest of NASCAR tracks was the speedway in Fonda, New York. The Fonda family had been killed during an Indian uprising around the time of the Revolutionary War and the family burial plot was located just outside the track's third turn. The Mohawk River also ran behind the backstretch and, occasionally, racers would wind up in the river.

The opening of Daytona International Speedway in 1959 also marked the beginning of a new era for NASCAR. Daytona was the first paved American superspeedway with high banks—the 31-degree banking rises five stories above the infield, which includes a road course.

Two of NASCAR's oldest active tracks are the paved oval at Greenville Pickens Speedway in Greenville, South Carolina, left, and Bowman Gray Stadium in Winston-Salem, North Carolina, which attracts packed houses for Modified races.

Each new track brought its own distinctive characteristics. Charlotte Motor Speedway opened in 1960 with a unique double dogleg front stretch that was copied by Texas Motor Speedway, which opened in 1997. Michigan Speedway's two-mile oval produced such fine racing that owner Roger Penske duplicated the design almost exactly for his new California Speedway in Fontana.

Over NASCAR's first half-century, the tracks have changed as much as the cars and the men driving them.

—*Jonathan V. Mauk*

"I'm kind of partial to Richmond. It brings back fond memories of the three some sort of roots there. The people are friendly. **Going back to Richmond**

years I raced for Junie Donlavey, whose team is based in Richmond. I feel I have

is like going home." —Driver Ken Schrader on the D-shaped, three-quarter-mile oval at Richmond, Virginia

Dale Jarrett wins the night race at Richmond, Virginia, on September 6, 1997.

TRIUMPH

Jeff Gordon is doused with champagne in the victory celebration following the 1997 Daytona 500.

"Winning is good. The first time I won, it felt great. The second time was better because I remembered how I felt the first time. So you know how I felt the third time. And winning the championship . . . I'll tell you how I feel when my head comes back down from the clouds."

—A euphoric Alan Kulwicki after winning the 1992 NASCAR Winston Cup Series championship

The legacy of Kulwicki, who is shown celebrating victory with a shower of confetti, below, lived on after his tragic death in an airplane crash in 1993. Geoff Bodine purchased Kulwicki's team and retained the crew. Crew chief Paul Andrews, right, leads the charge as the team celebrates a victory under Bodine at Watkins Glen, New York, on August 11, 1996.

"Sometimes I can't watch during the final laps. I know Jeff's going as fast as he can, but from where I am it's like everything is moving in slow motion. It's hard to watch."

—Kim Burton

Burton bursts into tears as husband Jeff crosses the finish line to win the inaugural race at Texas Motor Speedway on April 6, 1997.

The crowd was on its feet.

And so was the President of the United States of America.

The date was July 4, 1984, and it marked the ultimate moment of victory for NASCAR.

Richard Petty was winning his milestone 200th race. And on hand to cheer him to victory was none other than Ronald Reagan.

Talk about symbolic. NASCAR's King and the nation's President.

As Petty and Cale Yarborough bumped and swapped paint during their closing-laps dash to the finish, President Reagan was one of us. At the checkered flag, the Commander in Chief cheered.

A great moment. But in a way, not unlike the great moments of every other race NASCAR has run over fifty seasons.

What President Reagan experienced on that 208th anniversary of the nation's birth is not unlike what NASCAR fans experience weekly.

Every race has its winner. And when success continues, winners become champions . . . and champions legends.

For fifty years, the names have been heard loud and clear over the roar of the engines.

Petty. Earnhardt. Pearson. Weatherly. Allison. Gordon. Yarborough. Johnson. Jarrett. Kulwicki. Wallace. Martin. Labonte. Phillips. Evans. Cook. Ingram.

And more. Hundreds more. Thousands more. Great drivers. And drivers who raced the greats.

Without cars and tracks, there would be no racing. But it was the drivers who propelled NASCAR into the American sports psyche. "The champions of today and the winners of tomorrow will forever owe a debt to the guys who got it rolling," said Rusty Wallace while contemplating the modern driver's place in NASCAR history.

"More than cars, NASCAR racing is people," said Buddy Baker, one of the sport's second-generation drivers. People and eras.

The early winners became NASCAR's foundation. Lee Petty. Joe Weatherly. Buck Baker. Tim and Fonty Flock. Junior Johnson. "Fireball" Roberts. Curtis Turner. Herb Thomas.

Lee Petty, Richard's father, competed in the first NASCAR Strictly Stock race (now called the NASCAR Winston Cup Series) on June 19, 1949, at Charlotte, North Carolina. During the first decade of Grand National racing, Lee won more championships (three) and races (forty-nine) than anyone.

It was that wide-open first decade that established the competitive nature of NASCAR racing.

Cale Yarborough won the most contested race in NASCAR history on May 6, 1984, at Talladega Superspeedway. Yarborough was the 75th—and final—leader of the 500-mile battle.

It was truly a golden era that created a recurring pattern—one, two, or three drivers zooming to the top and then along comes another dozen trying to knock them from the pinnacle. This battle for supremacy takes place at every race, which is one reason fans flock to NASCAR events.

But NASCAR's dramatic history can also be split into eras during which certain drivers soared to the head of the pack. The cycles evolved smoothly and often overlapped.

As the 1950s ended and the 1960s began, it was "Fireball" Roberts, Junior Johnson, Joe Weatherly, Ned Jarrett, David Pearson, Fred Lorenzen, and a young Richard Petty trying to claim a spot among the sport's elite. By the time R. J. Reynolds Tobacco Co. had come on board as the NASCAR Winston Cup sponsor in 1971, Petty and Pearson were NASCAR's superstars. They would remain in this role throughout the 1970s as their rivalry treated the fans to some of the greatest races in the history of the sport, including the 1976 Daytona 500.

Petty and Pearson are the sport's all-time leaders in race wins. But as great as they were, the pair faced constant challenges as first Bobby Isaac and then Cale Yarborough, Bobby Allison, and Buddy Baker battled them for supremacy.

By the end of the 1970s, Yarborough had become the first driver to win three consecutive NASCAR Winston Cup Series championships and Petty had boosted his championship total to seven.

But two new stars were on the horizon—Darrell Waltrip and Dale Earnhardt. Waltrip would win three championships during the first half of the '80s. And Earnhardt would open that decade by claiming the first of his record-equalling seven titles.

In 1985, another new star was born—Bill Elliott. By winning three of the sport's four crown jewels—the Daytona 500, the Winston 500, and the Southern 500 (the fourth being the Coca-Cola 600)—Elliott won the Winston Million (a one-million-dollar bonus awarded by R. J. Reynolds) thus earning the nickname "Million-Dollar Bill."

The Winston Million feat wasn't repeated until Jeff Gordon did so in 1997. By that time, Gordon had already become the second-youngest NASCAR Winston Cup Series champion in history.

The decade between Elliott and Gordon was dominated by "the Intimidator" Earnhardt, who won his next six championships between 1986 and 1994. The other three titles went to Bill Elliott, Rusty Wallace, and Alan Kulwicki.

As the sport heads toward the 21st century, we are in the midst of the Jeff Gordon Era. Will Gordon be as dominant as Petty and Earnhardt? Or are we headed into another wide-open era such as the one that marked NASCAR's infancy?

—Bob Moore

"When Ralph Seagraves first came to me with this million dollar thing,

he told me no way anyone is going to win it.

He hadn't counted on Bill Elliott."

—Jerry Long, former president and CEO of R. J. Reynolds

Since 1971, RJR has been the title sponsor of NASCAR's Winston Cup Series. Beginning with the 1985 season, RJR has offered a $1 million bonus to a driver who wins three of NASCAR's four "crown jewels"—the Daytona 500 at Daytona International Speedway, the Winston 500 at Talladega Superspeedway, the Coca-Cola 600 at Charlotte Motor Speedway, and the Mountain Dew Southern 500 at Darlington Raceway. Bill Elliott won the $1 million the first time it was offered. Jeff Gordon was the second winner in 1997.

Bill Elliott accepts a nice bonus check and kiss after winning the Winston Million in 1985. At the podium, RJR's T. Wayne Robertson (right) is joined by NASCAR president Bill France Jr. during the 1996 annual NASCAR Winston Cup Series Awards Banquet. Enjoying a day at the North Carolina Motor Speedway, Ralph Seagraves (left) and T. Wayne Robertson pose for a picture.

Darrell Waltrip

Dale Earnhardt

Lee Petty

Ned Jarrett

Jack Ingram

Cale Yarborough

THE LEGENDS

The first couple of them trickled in, the legends, Larry then Jerry. The next four or five came in a spurt, one right after the other. Cale and Ned and Bobby and David and Junior. Hershel brought members of his family. So did Richard and Lee. They came with each other. Jack and Dale and then, finally, Darrell. They were all there. Thirteen of the greatest drivers ever to sit behind the wheel of a race car.

More than 50 championships and 2,500 wins in at least eight different divisions. They represent a span of fifty years. Fifty years of competition and magic. And when they came together in an empty race shop, the roar of all those engines and miles and the shouts of fans could be heard and it was magic again.

Richard Petty **Bobby Allison**

David Pearson **Hershel McGriff**

Larry Phillips **Junior Johnson**

Jerry Cook

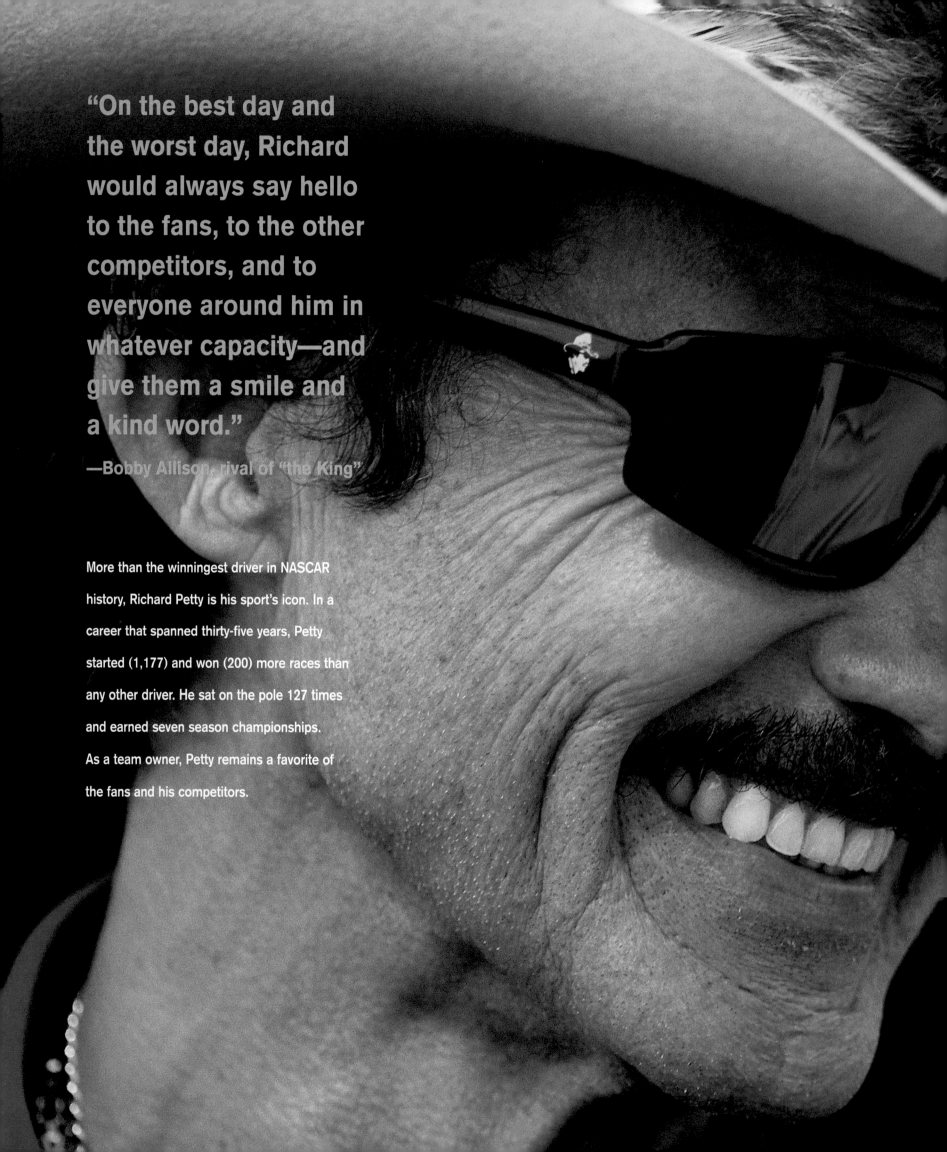

"On the best day and the worst day, Richard would always say hello to the fans, to the other competitors, and to everyone around him in whatever capacity—and give them a smile and a kind word."

—Bobby Allison, rival of "the King"

More than the winningest driver in NASCAR history, Richard Petty is his sport's icon. In a career that spanned thirty-five years, Petty started (1,177) and won (200) more races than any other driver. He sat on the pole 127 times and earned seven season championships. As a team owner, Petty remains a favorite of the fans and his competitors.

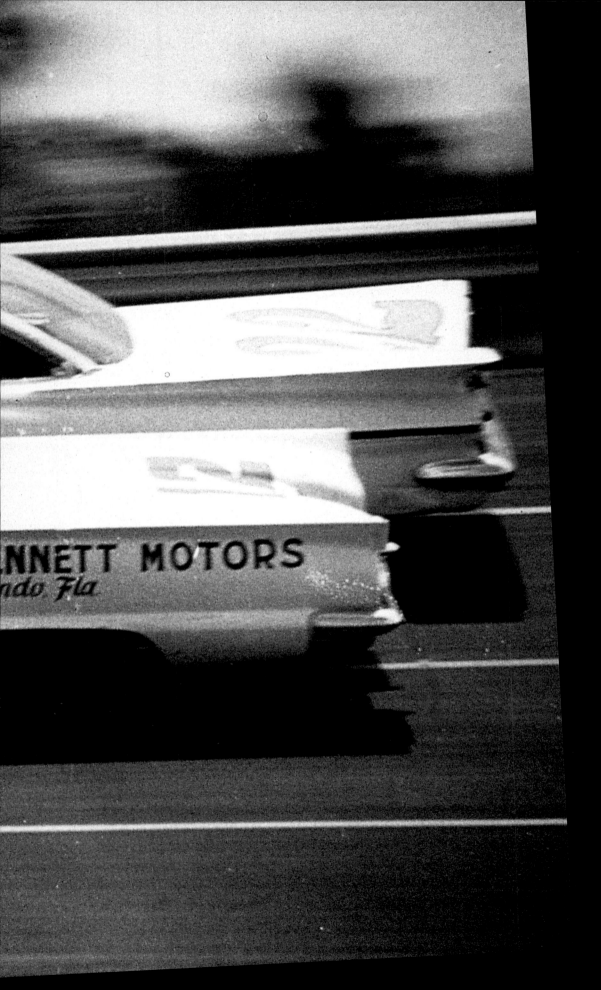

Quick-witted and fun-loving Joe Weatherly, shown here driving under Johnny Allen en route to a second-place finish in the 1959 Firecracker 250, coined the phrases "flat-out" and "belly to the ground" to describe a personality and a driving style that attracted fans to NASCAR in the early '60s. A motorcycle champion after World War II, Weatherly became one of NASCAR's first superstars. He won 101 Modified races in 1952–53 and the NASCAR Modified Division Championship in 1953. He also ran Convertibles in 1956 and joined the NASCAR Grand National Series in 1960. In addition to promoting the sport, Weatherly won back-to-back championships in 1962 and 1963, and a total of twenty-four NASCAR Grand National races during his career.

"David Pearson was one of the first real smart, calculating drivers. He took care of his equipment and knew when to race hard and when not to charge. **He made it look easy, but he worked hard at perfecting it."**

—Former NASCAR Winston Cup Series champion Ned Jarrett

David Pearson celebrates one of his record five Firecracker 400 wins at Daytona. Nicknamed "the Silver Fox" for his strategic genius behind the wheel, Pearson is number two on the all-time list of career NASCAR Winston Cup race winners with 105 victories. He won three season championships in 1966, 1968, and 1969.

"Darrell adds a sparkle to the race.

The media and television people love him because he is quick with a word.

And he wins races, which makes it even better."

—Car owner Junior Johnson

Darrell Waltrip has won eighty-four races and three NASCAR Winston Cup Series titles—including twelve wins and eleven poles in '81.

"**I've never seen anyone adapt to these cars as fast as Jeff Gordon.**
He's probably the most talented driver to come along in I don't know how long. You don't see someone
come in that young and with that little experience and do what he's done."

—1996 NASCAR Winston Cup Series champion Terry Labonte

Jeff Gordon was 26 when he won his second NASCAR Winston Cup Series championship in 1997. Richard Petty won his second title at the age of 30.

Dale Earnhardt was 35 when he won his second title. Over the last three seasons, Gordon has won 27 races.

"Cale Yarborough jumped in the car and pushed the gas pedal to the floor before he turned it on. When the green flag came out, he locked the throttle on 'kill,' and gritted his teeth and hung on. And he did that really well."

—Former NASCAR Winston Cup Series champion Bobby Allison

Yarborough is considered one of the hardest chargers in NASCAR history. He won eighty-three NASCAR Winston Cup races and is the only driver to win three straight season championships (1976, 1977, 1978).

"When you hear the name 'Earnhardt,' you know you're talking about the hardest driving, never-say-die competitor there is. He's one of the best drivers at taking a car and driving it past its limits, no matter how good or how bad it might be on any given day. That's what makes him 'the Intimidator.'"

—NASCAR Winston Cup driver Ted Musgrave

In 1994, Dale Earnhardt equalled one of Richard Petty's "untouchable" records by winning his seventh NASCAR Winston Cup Series championship. The son of Ralph Earnhardt, NASCAR's 1956 Sportsman Division champion, Earnhardt grew up around stock cars and developed a tenacious driving style. But Earnhardt, celebrating his triumph with wife Teresa at the 1994 NASCAR Winston Cup Series Awards Banquet in New York City, is equal parts racer, businessman, and family man.

"Red was an extra good driver. He'd get going about half-way through the to this day. Red was very smart, very shrewd . . . very hard to beat."

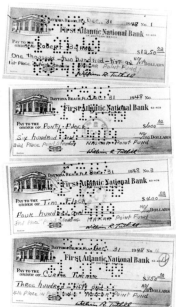

race. I think he'd stack up fine

—Car owner Raymond Parks on Red Byron

Red Byron, left, was NASCAR's first champion—
and much more. A popular and successful driver
after World War II, Byron backed Bill France's bid
to form a national sanctioning body for stock car
racing. Byron won NASCAR's first title in 1948 in
the Modified division. His share of the NASCAR
point fund was $1,250. Fonty Flock won $600 for finishing second, and his brother
Tim, above, was awarded $400 for placing third. Pictured at top, Curtis Turner took
home the fourth-place share of $350. A year later, driving an Oldsmobile for famed car
owner Raymond Parks and mechanic Red Vogt, Byron won the first NASCAR Strictly
Stock title—the forerunner of today's NASCAR Winston Cup Series.

"My father taught me the meaning of this race. This is the race the drivers

want to win. You want the Daytona 500 on your resume." —Davey Allison

Four years after running second to father Bobby in the Daytona 500, Davey Allison won in 1992 then shared the victory with wife Liz and the couple's two young children.

DEVOTION

The infield at any NASCAR Winston Cup event becomes a sea of motor homes complete with rooftop spectators.

"My favorite NASCAR memory is seeing my son's face the first time I took him to a NASCAR Winston Cup race. When the field roared past at 170 miles an hour, his face lit up."

—NASCAR fan Dick Childers, Atlanta, Georgia

Right, headsets and binoculars are the perfect accessories for a young fan at a NASCAR race. Below, a young fan proudly holds a souvenir flag from NASCAR's 1996 inaugural event in Suzuka, Japan.

92

"It's impossible to hide your emotions at a NASCAR race. The action demands you celebrate."
—NASCAR fan Gene Simmons of Portland, Oregon

A NASCAR fan displays his star-spangled devotion to his country.

As the black motor coach backed into its space on the infield at Daytona International Speedway, it drew a lot of attention.

"It's always tough with new neighbors," said Rich Lewis, sitting amid a dozen Bill Elliott flags on the roof of his motor home in an adjacent space. "You never know who they are going to favor."

Moments later, a lone figure dressed in black emerged from the black coach. Lewis and his friends fell silent. The breeze died and their Elliott flags fell slack.

The still was broken with the sound of another flag being raised. It was a red number 3 set against a black background.

"Earnhardt people," said Lewis. "There goes the neighborhood." Of course, the "neighborhood" at any NASCAR event is an eclectic community. The United Nations would be envious of the variety of flags flying in the infield.

Every driver in the sport has a legion of partisans. And the link between a NASCAR fan and a favorite driver is easy to see but often hard to describe.

The relationship between drivers, their fans, and their communities is one of appreciation, care, and loyalty.

"I love them and they love me. It is as easy as that," a champion driver once said while describing the union between him and his followers. "Without them, I'm not Richard Petty."

"We are an extension of our fans," said Terry Labonte. "It's never like I'm out there by myself. You can always feel them pulling for you."

There is a strong interpersonal link between the NASCAR Winston Cup drivers and those who support them that is, perhaps, unmatched in any other sport.

"What amazes me most about NASCAR fans is how personal they can get with you," said Ray Evernham, crew chief for the No. 24 DuPont Chevrolet. "Things like the illness to my son and the illness with [team owner] Rick Hendrick. It's amazing how supportive people can be."

Each NASCAR fan is totally devoted to one chosen driver. There can be no other appropriate way to say it. The fan becomes immersed in the driver's career and follows it with rapt attention—and does considerably more than that.

Fences at speedways are lined with fans clamoring for autographs. Drivers' personal appearances are mob scenes.

The devotion doesn't stop there.

The burgeoning popularity of NASCAR racing has allowed the competitors to license their names and likenesses to innumerable products—from hats and T-shirts to trading cards, key rings, binoculars, and much more.

Souvenir rigs featuring products related to nearly all of the NASCAR Winston Cup drivers create a market-like atmosphere at every speedway. The business, needless to say, is very brisk.

NASCAR fans robe themselves with the signature clothes of their favorites. Motor homes parked in the infield raise the banners of selected drivers.

"We're Ernie Irvan people," Robert Brooks of Richmond, Virginia, said before a recent race. "Over there, you got your Earnhardt people and your Jeff Gordon people. We can share a soda or coffee or a beer. But it's not likely that we'll get together during the race."

With spectators lining both sides of the track, Ricky Craven charges into the main straight on the road course at Watkins Glen, New York.

The fans are loyal because the drivers are loyal to the sport.

"Why do I love NASCAR Winston Cup racing?" wondered Tim Largent of Los Angeles during the first race at the new California Speedway. "The drivers act more like regular people than celebrities."

So the drivers give in return. And giving doesn't stop with autographs. NASCAR Winston Cup drivers feel a sense of responsibility to community. Drivers are well aware of the fans' devotion, knowing that it is indeed the foundation of their careers. So they respond by giving back whenever possible.

"If there is one thing a driver new to NASCAR Winston Cup racing is taught," said Kyle Petty, "it's that you never, never charge for an autograph. You have to realize that it's the fans who are allowing you to make a living doing what you love. So you give back something."

—Steve Waid

"What's not to love?

The roar of the engines, the race—not only for first but for fifteenth,

the smell of burning rubber, the speed of the pit crews, and the great drivers that made

NASCAR what it is. Earnhardt, Petty, the Allisons.

I love that roar and the thrill of standing by the fence as the cars roll by."

—NASCAR fan Beth Bland of West Allis, Wisconsin

Fans partisan to the infield begin arriving more than two days before NASCAR races to claim top spots alongside the track. Some infield compounds are no more elaborate than a pickup truck and lawn chairs. Some motor homes come complete with hot tubs. The fortified roof of a motor home offers some of the best viewing.

"NASCAR is the fans . . . the most loyal, hospitable, and friendliest. You go to any track in your 'fan gear' and a complete stranger will come up to you, start a conversation, . . . and you've just made a friend."

—NASCAR fan Scott White, Newtown, Connecticut

Action in the grandstands and in the infield during a NASCAR weekend is a potpourri of activity, including, for Lorraine and Colin Smith of Longwood, Florida, their wedding atop a motor home on the eve of the 1997 Pepsi 400 at Daytona International Speedway.

"We're the Davids vs. Goliaths . . . I'm so proud of this team. I came to winning a race on this track. I didn't dream it would ever happen. And

Rudd, who has owned his team since 1994, celebrates with his crew after driving his Ford to victory in the 1997 Brickyard 400 before more than 300,000 spectators at

Indianapolis in 1971 to race go-karts and I started dreaming about here I am. This is incredible." —Owner/driver Ricky Rudd

the famed Indianapolis Motor Speedway. Rudd, whose father owned some of his earliest cars, has scored at least one victory per season in fifteen straight seasons.

There was a time in NASCAR racing when the cars were the stars.

"Win on Sunday, sell on Monday" was a popular slogan with automotive executives and salesmen.

And there were plenty of makes to sell in the formative years.

The thirty-three cars lined up for the first NASCAR Strictly Stock race in 1949 included Lincolns, Hudsons, Oldsmobiles, Fords, Buicks, Chryslers, Kaisers, a Mercury, and even a Cadillac. All those plus Plymouths, Nashes, and Studebakers were on hand a year

BUILT FOR SPEED   later for the first superspeedway event.

The dominant cars in the early years were big, sturdy, boxlike Hudson Hornets, especially those driven by Marshall Teague and Herb Thomas, who claimed two championships in a Hudson. The Hudsons were about as aerodynamic as a barn door, but the cars could take a lot of punishment and had a very low center of gravity, which enabled them to corner well.

In the mid '50s, the powerful Chrysler 300s reigned for the team owned by Carl Kiekhaefer, also the developer of Mercury outboard motors. His star drivers, Tim Flock and Buck Baker, both won titles. "Chrysler 300s made terrific race cars," said Flock. "The main thing was the engines. They came ready to race." The next dominant car was the classic '57 Chevy—rated by some as the best-looking American car ever built. Baker gave Chevrolet its first championship in a '57 Chevy.

The most exotic NASCAR machines were the Dodge Daytonas and Plymouth Superbirds of 1969–1970. The cars were distinguished by needle-nose grills and "wings" jutting high up from the rear deck lids. "They seemed so futuristic that you almost imagined yourself as an astronaut in a rocket getting ready to blast off into space," said Baker. "The lines of the car gave you a feeling of superiority." Another trend was set by the fastback Mercury Cyclones and Ford Torinos of the late '60s, which were aerodynamically advanced decades before the term became popular.

It was Richard Petty who shifted the emphasis from the cars to the men behind the wheel. "The King" switched from Oldsmobile to Plymouth to Ford to Dodge to Chevrolet and finally to Pontiac over a thirty-five seasons—and his legion of fans went along for the ride. The turning point might have come during the summer of 1978 when Petty made a controversial midseason switch from Dodge to Chevrolet. There were fears that

Dodge supporters would revolt against their idol. But the fans cheered as hard for Petty in a Chevy as they had when he was driving a Dodge. And drivers began moving to the forefront of the sport.

NASCAR still features car wars. But the battles are expanding. Today there are trucks as well as cars competing in NASCAR. Ford, Chevrolet, and Dodge all compete in the young NASCAR Craftsman Truck Series.

—Tom Higgins

The "winged" Dodge Daytonas and Plymouth Superbirds were crowd favorites in 1969 and 1970.

"The cars were still pretty stock when I stopped racing in 1956. They had everything in them.

Glove box, cigarette lighter, radio. You could listen to the radio during the race."

—Two-time NASCAR Winston Cup champion Herb Thomas

Herb Thomas, top, waves to the crowd from behind the wheel of his Hudson Hornet that was far from aerodynamic. In contrast, the fastback

Mercury Cyclones driven here by Bobby Allison, above, and Ford Torinos were among the first aerodynamically advanced cars of the late '60s.

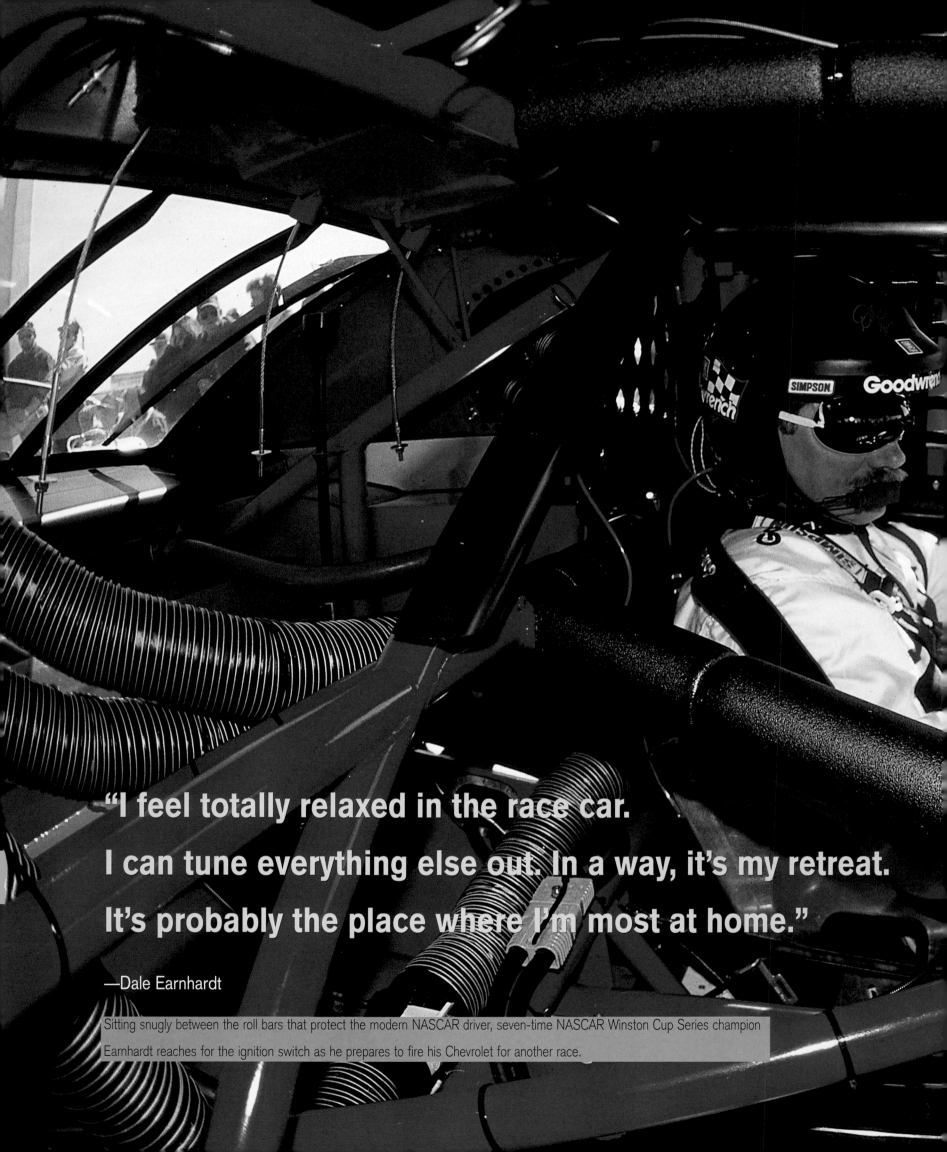

"I feel totally relaxed in the race car.
I can tune everything else out. In a way, it's my retreat.
It's probably the place where I'm most at home."

—Dale Earnhardt

Sitting snugly between the roll bars that protect the modern NASCAR driver, seven-time NASCAR Winston Cup Series champion
Earnhardt reaches for the ignition switch as he prepares to fire his Chevrolet for another race.

"We're NASCAR people. We raise kids and work hard all soccer and baseball. Sundays are for racing. If we're not

—NASCAR fan Eddie Atkins of Atlanta, Georgia

week for a nice home. Saturdays are for chores and kids'
at the track, we're in front of the television."

Richard Petty was "thumbs up" for two
of the greatest moments of his career . . .
which were also milestone events for NASCAR.
As Petty races down the backstretch at Daytona
International Speedway on July 4, 1984, right,
Air Force One, carrying President Ronald Reagan,
lands in the background. For the first time
in history a President of the United States
was on hand to witness the finish of a NASCAR race.
Petty capped the celebration by winning the record
200th race of his career.
Below, Petty sits in the cockpit, as he
prepares to start the 1,177th and final race
of his thirty-five-year career.

you'd dreamed about put in one package and gift-wrapped so beautifully that you hated to open it."

—Richard Petty

"After fifty years this sport still brings out the enthusiasm and emotions of one's youth."

—Jim France, NASCAR Executive Vice President and Secretary

"My dad was a car guy. When he worked in the garage,

I'd sit in the driver's seat of the family's Ford. He'd give me the key so I could honk the horn

and it would drive my mom crazy. He took me to my first race, maybe my first ten races.

I remember that every time I go to a race."

—NASCAR fan Mike Stewart of Dallas, Texas

The father-son bond is a strong part of NASCAR racing, above.

As a boy in 1947, Jim France, opposite, reads a racing magazine on the porch of the family home.

Drivers like Ken Schrader and Bobby Allison always saw it as a chance to spread the word.

Run a NASCAR Winston Cup race on Sunday, make a midweek appearance for the fans the following Wednesday or Thursday, race at an out-of-the-way oval on Friday or Saturday . . . then hustle back to the major leagues.

They didn't have to run eighty races a year. They wanted to.

"If I could, I'd race every day," Schrader said recently. "I love the racing. I enjoy getting into a different car at a track I've never seen before—just to see what I can do. . . .

"And I enjoy the reaction of the fans when my name is announced at a place they wouldn't expect a NASCAR Winston

FOR THE LOVE OF RACING

Cup driver to be. It's rewarding to everyone."

You don't have to look very hard to find drivers who have given as much as they have received from the sport. NASCAR's history is rich with such drivers. There was a time when it wasn't unusual for drivers to race four and five times a week.

Dave Marcis is considered the last of the "old-time" independent drivers. He has spent three decades racing at the NASCAR Winston Cup level, mostly in cars he owned. Only Richard Petty has started more races than Marcis. But while "the King" had two hundred wins and seven titles, Marcis has five wins and no titles.

"I can't say that it hasn't been hard at times," Marcis said. "But I won't *ever* say it hasn't been fun."

In times of need, rivals rally to help drivers like Marcis. When he had engine problems early in 1997, none other than car owner Richard Childress and driver Dale Earnhardt came to Marcis's aid.

J. D. McDuffie started 653 races in his NASCAR Winston Cup career. Never won a single race. But McDuffie was a favorite with fans.

Most NASCAR Winston Cup drivers moved up through the ranks—advancing from local tracks to a NASCAR touring series. Geoff Bodine, for example, was a Modified champ. Many drivers, Mike Stefanik being a notable example, still prefer racing in multiple series and campaigning two and three days a week.

Bobby Allison understands that driving desire.

"I don't do it just for the fans at the small tracks," Allison once explained while visiting a midwestern oval. "I do it for me, too. The small tracks are my roots."

J. D. McDuffie was a winner with the fans.

Veteran campaigner Dave Marcis has dedicated a large part of his life to NASCAR racing.

"It's guys like Dave Marcis

who pour their heart and soul into it

that make racing what it is."

—Dale Earnhardt

"We can cheer.

**We can jump up and
down and hoot and
holler until our
lungs explode.

Do that in a grandstand seat
and they haul you away."**

—NASCAR fan Louisa Stanton
of Detroit, Michigan, on life in the infield

FAMILY

The top of a motor home with a pair of lawn chairs is the perfect viewing platform for a fan and his son during a NASCAR weekend.

Driver Ricky Craven shares a kiss with daughter Riley Diane before a drivers' meeting.

Stock car racing was desperately in need of a patriarch's firm hand fifty years ago.

In its formative stages, the sport was loosely controlled by independent promoters, some of whose operations were dubious at best.

"Sometimes you'd win the race, then have to beat the promoter to the back gate to be sure you got paid," Junior Johnson reminisced about some of the not-so-good old days.

"You might be the fastest car on the track, but that promoter was quicker than lightnin'."

Bill France changed that with the formation of NASCAR.

He brought order to chaos. More important, he gave stock car racing a unifying structure that thrives to this day. It was more than organization. It was a family approach—a sense that the common good takes precedence over individual goals.

To this day, NASCAR operates largely as an extended family directed by the heirs of Bill France Sr.

And families under the NASCAR umbrella have thrived and flourished—great racing families like the Pettys, Allisons, Flocks, Bakers, Bodines, Labontes, Waltrips, and Earnhardts.

At its highest level, NASCAR has had twelve sets of father/son drivers and seventeen sets of siblings. Presently there are six sets of brothers active on the NASCAR Winston Cup circuit—Brett, Geoff, and Todd Bodine; Jeff and Ward Burton; David and Jeff Green; Bobby and Terry Labonte; Kenny, Mike, and Rusty Wallace; and Darrell and Michael Waltrip.

Strong family ties extend throughout NASCAR's racing series. But the sense of family extends well beyond the NASCAR organization and its drivers and crews.

"I've never viewed fans as customers," California Speedway executive vice president Les Richter said recently at the opening of Roger Penske's new superspeedway east of Los Angeles. "Anyone who comes through our gates is part of our family."

The feel of family can be found in every aspect of NASCAR racing. As competitors travel around the country to race, their families have developed what amounts to a deep kinship within a fraternity that includes fans as well as drivers and crew.

The family connections are too numerous to chronicle. But there are some notable combinations.

The Wood Brothers are an example. Glen Wood owns and leads the team in which his sons, Len and Eddie, are key members. Glen's brother, Leonard, is the operation's longtime mechanical master; his daughter Kim Wood Hall runs the business end of the operation.

Doug Yates builds engines for the highly regarded teams owned by his dad, Robert Yates. Bill Elliott's engine builder is his brother, Ernie. Both Buddy Parrott and his son, Todd, are successful NASCAR Winston Cup crew chiefs, as are brothers Robin and Ryan Pemberton.

Marlene Smith co-owns a NASCAR Craftsman truck with her husband, Jim who helped develop the division's prototype.

It is quite a lengthy list.

Why so much family participation in the sport?

"I trace having the courage to drive a car very, very fast to heredity," says Dick Beaty, the highly regarded former NASCAR Winston Cup director. "The rest of it probably is environment, being around racing and cultivating a craving to be a part of it."

Generally, NASCAR competitors have assisted each other through the organization's five decades as they would "blood relations," says Beaty.

"Back in the old days, the drivers and what help they had as crewmen would stay up late, tuning and tinkering and patching up sheet metal. If guys had bad problems, everyone pitched in to get the cars ready for the next day. It always amazed me to then see them go out and try to beat each others' fannies off."

Such rivalry, unusual in most professional sports, has continued.

In 1991, Bobby Hamilton and Ted Musgrave were locked in a tight chase for the NASCAR Winston Cup Rookie of the Year title. Prior to a race at Pocono, Pennsylvania, Hamilton's team wound up needing a critical part for the car. Musgrave's team provided it. Hamilton narrowly won the rookie competition and its $50,000 bonus.

The Pettys are the winningest family on the track. But the first family racing was the Flocks, who outnumbered the Pettys three to one in NASCAR's first Strictly Stock race.

Brothers Bob, Fonty, and Tim Flock were entrants in the Strictly Stock inaugural. Twice later that season, they were joined on the grid by a sister, Ethel Flock Mobley.

The "Flying Flocks" are the only trio of brothers to win at NASCAR's highest level and, in 1952, they beat incredible odds to triumph in successive races—Bob at Syracuse, New York; Tim at Asheville-Weaverville; and Fonty at Darlington.

No family comes remotely close, however, to matching the Petty success. Three generations of Pettys have won more than 260 races in careers that have spanned NASCAR's half-century. Lee won fifty-four races and three championships before injuries forced his retirement in 1964. Richard succeeded his father and won two hundred races in a thirty-five-year career. Kyle continues the family tradition of winning at the NASCAR Winston Cup level.

While the Pettys have 149 more victories than the Allisons—brothers Bobby and Donnie, and Bobby's late son Davey—the most memorable "family finish" in NASCAR history belongs to the Allisons. Bobby fought off a spirited charge by Davey to win the 1988 Daytona 500, the son drafting his dad across the finish.

—Tom Higgins

"There's a time for everything—the fans, the media, and the family.

Keep the family close and everything will fall into place."

—Bill Elliott, twelve-time winner of the "Most Popular Driver" Award

Bill, Cindy, and Chase Elliott spend a few moments together prior to a race.

"He helped me from day one. Not just in racing, but in life in general. We

communicate and relate to each other."

—Bobby Labonte on brother Terry

"He does a good job and he's really worked at it. I've probably helped him a little. But when you get to this level, I really don't know how much you can help somebody. You're pretty much on your own. He's probably got more racing talent. After all, I taught him everything I know."

—Terry Labonte on brother Bobby

123

November 10, 1996, at Atlanta Motor Speedway marked a great day in the lives of the Labonte brothers of Corpus Christi, Texas. Above, Bobby maneuvers around brother Terry en route to victory in the season-ending Napa 500. Terry finished fifth to win his second NASCAR Winston Cup Series championship.

Ned Jarrett (left) won fifty races and two NASCAR Grand National titles as a driver. As a television commentator in 1993, Jarrett became "choked up" when he announced his son Dale's (right) winning of the Daytona 500—a victory that had eluded Ned.

Jeff (left) and Ward Burton (right) make up one of the newer brother acts on the NASCAR Winston Cup circuit.

Ernie Elliott (left) builds engines for the Ford driven by brother Bill (right).

"On the track, I don't know if there's

a lot of brotherly love going on.

But it's been great, particularly early in my career, that

I could bounce things off Darrell and know that he understood."

—Michael Waltrip on his relationship with brother Darrell

Brothers (left to right) Bob, Tim, and Fonty Flock all raced in NASCAR's formative years.

Their sister, Ethel Flock Mobley, was one of ten women to compete in NASCAR's top series.

"He's a superstar in the sport. But around the garages,
Yes, he wants to win. He wants to win for all of us."

Not always "the Intimidator," Earnhardt relaxes with crew members between practice sessions.

he's like one of the guys. Dale's a team player.

—Crew chief Larry McReynolds

"This is our family sport and everyone in the family roots for a different driver.

I'm a Mark Martin fan. The kids pull for Bobby and Terry Labonte and Kyle Petty. It makes for

very interesting dinner conversation. We go round and round in our opinions of cars, crew chiefs,

pit stops, and owners. NASCAR brings our family together." —NASCAR fan Judith Scott, Colonia, New Jersey

The capacity crowd at Phoenix International Raceway, left and above, spends much of the afternoon on its feet as Dale Jarrett wins the Dura Lube 500 on November 2, 1997.

They are the first family of the National Association for Stock Car Auto Racing. The France name and NASCAR go together like fireworks and the Fourth of July. The France family has been a motorsports tradition for fifty years.

It all started with the late patriarch, William H. G. (he was always known as "Big Bill" due to his 6' 5", 240 lb. frame) France, and wife Anne Bledsoe (she was always known as "Anne B."). This hard-working American family focused its undivided attention and energy—not to mention family financial resources—into first developing, and then maintaining, what is so popularly known today as America's most successful motorsports sanctioning group.

The NASCAR Winston Cup Series championship serves today as the organization's "marquee" series. It was Big Bill France's extraordinary vision to establish a "points" system for crowning a champion at the end of each season, culminating today with the annual December NASCAR Winston Cup Series Awards Banquet in the Grand Ballroom of New York's famed Waldorf-Astoria Hotel.

Big Bill France played the pivotal role from the very beginning of NASCAR, at a 1947 organizational meeting in Daytona Beach, where corporate headquarters has remained ever since. It was Big Bill's vision to develop a concept for racing stock cars, American-made family sedans like those used for everyday transportation by hard-working Americans—sometimes called showroom stock cars.

It was Big Bill's intention to create a sanctioning body and he did everything in his power to make it happen. He had a lot of support from other racing pioneers such as Joe Littlejohn, Alvin Hawkins, Red Vogt, Bill Tuthill, Sammy Packard, Tom Gallen, Frank Mundy, Eddie Bland, Harvey Tattersall, Marshall Teague, Buddy Shuman, Bob Richards, and Bob Osiecki. Many of these men are today enshrined along with France in stock car racing's National Motorsports Press Association Hall of Fame at Darlington, South Carolina.

It was also France's all-consuming energy and devotion, as well as Anne B.'s steady behind-the-scenes support, that kept NASCAR afloat during its turbulent, formative years. France's dedication and common-sense approach earned respect wherever he traveled, a respect that had grown worldwide by the time of his death in 1992.

Big Bill and Anne B. "grew" with NASCAR, while two sons, William C. and James C., "grew up" in the sport. Both Bill Jr. and Jim watched their parents overcome innumerable problems trying to manage NASCAR's day-to-day operations while also founding and funding both Daytona International Speedway (1959) and Talladega Superspeedway (1969). The two sons had experienced a broad-based view of NASCAR by the time they were old enough to understand that theirs was a business unlike any other.

Today's first family of NASCAR, opposite, includes (clockwise from top) Jim France, Bill France Jr., Bill's wife, Betty Jane, son Brian, daughter Lesa, and Jim's wife, Sharon. The original France family, right, included (clockwise from top) "Big Bill" France Sr., Anne B., Bill Jr., and Jim.

Bill France Sr. and Bill France Jr. on the beach at Daytona

When his parents started the Daytona International Speedway project, Bill Jr. had returned from a stint in the Navy and joined construction efforts. He learned to operate heavy equipment; how much concrete and asphalt cost; how much dirt had to be moved to create a superspeedway; how water, sewer, phone, and power lines were laid and how much they cost.

Jim was still in school. Nonetheless, both brothers, by the time they finished formal schooling, had experienced how NASCAR and its speedways interact. Jim's only absence from the family was a tour of duty in the Army.

Bill Jr. has served as NASCAR's president since 1972 with Jim at his side as executive vice president and secretary. They are both heavily involved in another lucrative business their father also founded, International Speedway Corporation (ISC), which currently owns racetracks across the country. Their on-the-job NASCAR and speedway training before Big Bill turned the reins over included learning a stock car and its parts and pieces inside-out, digging ditches, posting advertising flyers, managing budgets, selling tickets, parking cars, directing traffic, wiping off seats, inspecting race cars, driving a water wagon (many of NASCAR's early tracks were dirt and had to be watered to hold down the dust), analyzing rules, settling disputes, and just about anything else anyone can think of in the motorsports business. The France brothers have done it ALL. NASCAR's continuing success tells the world they've done it WELL.

The relationship between the brothers is one of the obvious strengths to NASCAR's success. Their number one priority is to get the job done. Bill Jr., by seniority, sits in the pilot's seat while Jim is perfectly content in the copilot's seat. There has never been any sibling rivalry between the two. Primarily, they genuinely respect each other. Anne B.'s pragmatism rubbed off to the extent that neither brother takes time to worry about what the other is doing because he's so busy himself.

Now, there's a third generation of France family members—Bill Jr. and wife Betty Jane's son, Brian, and daughter, Lesa France Kennedy; as well as Jim and wife Sharon's son, Jamie, and daughters, Jennifer and Amy.

They have also learned the ropes the same way their fathers and grandparents learned them—hands-on. Brian heads up NASCAR's marketing and licensing departments, which are responsible for projects such as the NASCAR Cafe restaurants, NASCAR Thunder retail stores, and NASCAR's Web site, NASCAR Online. Jamie France is also involved in NASCAR's marketing group.

Lesa Kennedy has worked her way up through the business to the executive vice president role at ISC. She is also credited as the mastermind behind Daytona USA, the ultimate motorsports attraction, located in Daytona Beach, Florida.

The France family is, indeed, committed to maintaining what Big Bill and Anne B. laid as the foundation fifty years ago, and they remain the first family of NASCAR.

—*Hunter James*

Bill France Jr. with wife Betty Jane play with their children Brian and Lesa.

"I always felt that we had something

that would interest so many people.

The public has a basic interest in cars.

And when you get a good thing going,

you don't change it."

—Bill France Sr.

Bill France raced stock cars prior to forming NASCAR in 1948.

The ear-to-ear grin always has come naturally; the sunglasses, the snakeskin-wrapped ten-gallon hat, and the cowboy boots were given some thought.

Over the years, the garb as much as the electric—some folks would say Carolina—blue STP-sponsored race cars have become synonymous with "the King" and his court, à la Petty Enterprises.

No NASCAR Winston Cup driver has ever been as successful or made as positive an impact as Richard Petty, who followed in Papa Lee's tire tracks to become "the King."

But the Petty story goes beyond one man—even if that man is considered by some to be the greatest driver in the history of NASCAR racing.

The Pettys—starting with patriarch Lee, sons Richard and Maurice, their cousin Dale Inman, and Richard's son Kyle—are an American racing family. The Pettys did more than win races—and they've won more than 260. They set a tone for NASCAR racing and drivers—inside and outside the car.

"I don't know of anything specifically that we have done to make the sport take off to where it is today," Richard said as he stretched out on a couch in his lush motor home. "I know Daddy was there at the first Strictly Stock race [at a Charlotte short track in 1949] and we have progressed all the way through till now. What we've contributed, I guess, is some stability from our end of it, so we all could make a living out of it. And trying to show it as a family sport. I think we did that to begin with and I think we still do that, and it shows all the way through the whole deal.

"As far as what we did to help it or anything like that, we came along and went along with whatever the show was. We tried to improve it in our own little ways. I don't know of any major things. But I guess we realized, basically, to begin with, that the fans were paying the bills. The whole Petty organization realized that and I think they've always looked at that part of it. They've been very fan-oriented and I think everybody else saw the same thing."

Through good times and tough times, the Pettys endured. They rolled with punches as well as celebrated victories. More than being one of NASCAR's pioneer drivers, Lee was one of the sport's first stars. He won fifty-four races and three championships. He formed Petty Enterprises, which operates to this day under Richard's guidance. Richard was also there when Papa Lee drove a car to that first NASCAR Strictly Stock race, rolled it during the race . . . then drove it home.

A decade later, at the age of twenty-two, Richard was the NASCAR Grand National Rookie of the Year, launching a career that spanned thirty-five seasons, producing scores of unbreakable records. Richard Petty won seven championships, a mark equalled only by Dale Earnhardt.

And the Petty family rode shotgun with "the King." After a short driving career of his own, Maurice became Richard's engine builder, and Dale Inman, his crew chief. Kyle continues the Petty tradition as an owner/driver and his son Adam has launched his own career in the NASCAR Late Model Sportsman Division.

—*Gerald Martin*

"Adam might go on for another thirty years.

It's possible that when the sport is around for seventy-five or eighty years

there will be a Petty in every one."

—Third-generation driver Kyle Petty on son Adam

Head west out of Virginia's Patrick County and there's no way to go but up . . . into the lush Blue Ridge, speckled with mountain laurel and rhododendron, narrow, gurgling creeks, and a roadside overlook called Lovers' Leap.

And there at the foot of the mountain, in the small town of Stuart, is where it all began in barely more than a woodshed, hard against one of those creeks that overran the banks and ebbed with every thundering storm.

The Wood Brothers, Glen and Leonard, have been turning out winning NASCAR Winston Cup race cars while maintaining a lifestyle that can only be termed "enviable."

Like Junior Johnson down in Wilkes County, North Carolina, the Wood Brothers never left their mountain roots for

WOOD BROTHERS

high-buck digs around Charlotte, though their small garage has been abandoned for an elaborate racing stable that now—in the capable hands of Glen's sons, Eddie and Len, and Leonard's daughter, Kim—continues to produce some of the most competitive cars in NASCAR Winston Cup competition.

Since 1950, the brothers and their kin were known as the noncussing, nonsmoking, nondrinking, churchgoing clan, bound and determined to do it their way and to do it as good as or better than the rest. Ninety-six victories later, it's quite evident that they did a lot of things the right way. Their stable of oval-track drivers has included the likes of Curtis Turner, David Pearson, Cale Yarborough, Buddy Baker, Kyle Petty, and Michael Waltrip. And across the country, on the West Coast, they built Riverside road course winners for Dan Gurney and Parnelli Jones.

Although content to compete in a limited number of races rather than run every year for the championship, the Wood Brothers, with Pearson at the wheel, won eleven of eighteen races in 1973 and ten of twenty-two in 1976.

And it all began with "the Woodchopper," as patriarch Glen was called during his driving days. Glen and master mechanic engine whiz Leonard did it their way from the very beginning at Bowman Gray Stadium in Winston-Salem, North Carolina. In the ensuing years, the Wood Brothers would leave an indelible mark on their sport and revolutionize some aspects of NASCAR racing—most notably, pit stops.

"In 1960, we decided there was a lot of time that could be gained in the pits, and we started working really hard at speeding up pit stops," Leonard said. "I remember Smokey Yunick's car: 'Fireball' Roberts was driving it in Charlotte, and he came in and I believe it was forty-five seconds they stayed in the pits. Well, we got to looking at pit stops . . . if you gained time there, it would be gained time on the racetrack. We practiced [pit stops], we made changes to the air guns and our jacks. When we first started making faster [pit stops], we would come out a half-lap ahead. But it didn't take long for the other guys to see what was happening and they started doing it also."

In NASCAR, the Wood Brothers set the standard for teamwork. —*Gerald Martin*

The Wood brothers still like to keep on top—and inside—of the engines of their winning cars. Glen (left of the engine) and Leonard (right) have passed along their love of racing to Glen's sons, Len (far left) and Eddie, and Leonard's daughter, Kim Wood Hall.

"Jordan loves being at the track. This is where she has friends and playmates. For me, it's exciting to have Jordan and Kim at the racetrack. It means more when I win to have them there to share it with me."

—NASCAR Winston Cup driver Ernie Irvan

Right, Jeff Gordon jokes with Jordan Irvan as dad Ernie looks on. Below, Darrell and Stevie Waltrip walk along pit lane in Watkins Glen, New York, in 1997 with daughters Sarah, left, and Jessica.

The right-side tires changed, Bill Elliott's crew hustles to complete a pit stop during the 1997 Mountain Dew Southern 500 at Darlington, South Carolina.

TEAMWORK

As the team's pit sign is lowered, Jeff Gordon's "Rainbow Warriors" crew looks up pit lane while anxiously awaiting the arrival of the No. 24 car.

Ray Evernham knew what he was missing. Talent.
Jeff Gordon knew what he needed. A coach.

"That day we met in 1990, Jeff and I hit it off," Evernham says. "I think each of us holds the missing part that the other needs. We both had goals but didn't know how to achieve them. The instant we met, it was like the last piece was there.

"I had the desire and the knowledge, I just didn't have the talent. Jeff did. I'm a good coach. I feel like I can bring out the best in Jeff Gordon and the best in the crew. In turn, they bring out the best in me."   **TOGETHER WE ROCK**

That is the essence of teamwork. And teamwork is the backbone of NASCAR racing.

It might look like it's man-and-machine vs. man-and-machine out there. But nothing could be farther from the truth. NASCAR is a team sport.

The work never ends. Left, a crewman hurries four tires from the Goodyear compound to the pits. Center, a member of Bobby Labonte's crew maintains diligence during a practice session. Right, crews scramble to top gas tanks and clean windshields during a rain delay.

Ever wonder why the same cars invariably charge to the front in the closing laps of a grueling five-hundred-mile race?

The winning combination in NASCAR racing starts with the relationship between the driver and crew chief. Evernham is considerably more than Gordon's crew chief. Having worked with the young superstar since their NASCAR Busch Series days, Evernham is equal parts adviser, friend, partner, and cheerleader.

"It used to be that I tried to keep Jeff settled down," says Evernham. "Now, more often, I think it's Jeff who keeps me under control."

They live out the triumphs and the failures together, these two. Gordon's performance reflects a young man of deceptive toughness. He never gives up. Anyone who listens to Evernham's coaching understands why.

But they are only as strong as the team they are leading.

The secret of a winning team is found in the relationship between the crew chief, his driver, and an organization that includes engine builders, fabricators, mechanics, truck drivers, public relations experts, receptionists, and others.

Crew chiefs such as Evernham, Steve Hmiel, and Robin Pemberton seem to have dual effects on the many employees under them. On the one hand, they are calming—knowing that additional pressure will only aggravate the frantic atmosphere of a pit row. At the same time, they are inspirational, example-setting leaders, always ready to take the criticism, deflect the blame, and pass along the credit to the foot soldiers.

"It is so hard to keep everybody working together," says Ricky Rudd, who balances the demands of being a driver and car owner.

"When you're building a race team, you have to put a lot of thought into it and use a lot of judgment in matching together people who like each other, who have the desire to do what it takes for success.

"You've got to be sensitive to the effect of a heavy workload on people. No one can run on empty forever.

"What has made that even more difficult is the fact that it's harder to keep that unit together. There are so many teams, and so many races, and the sport has become so popular, that there is a lot of pressure for a person on your team to move elsewhere, whether he's drawn to another team by its success, more money, or whatever.

Pit stops are as old as NASCAR. Left, the Wood Brothers, shown working on David Pearson's Mercury in 1976, revolutionized the sport with their quick pit stops. Center, tires are easily accessible on a modified. Right, pit stops were conducted at a more leisurely pace during the races on Daytona's Beach-Road course.

"A lot of times you feel like you're taking a step backward for every one you move ahead."

The prime example of teamwork is the pit stop—that deft maneuver, repeated hundreds of times a season, in which six men jump over the wall, refuel the car, and replace worn rubber in less time than it takes an Olympic sprinter to run two hundred meters.

While the pit stop epitomizes the cohesiveness of a championship team, it is but the tip of the iceberg. And the key is communication.

In an age in which a quarter of an inch makes a measurable difference in the lap speed of a NASCAR Winston Cup car, teamwork still remains the most important factor between winning and losing.

—*Monty Dutton*

"I love the teamwork of the sport, the physics involved in getting the car to handle just right.

This sport is more than engines.

These guys are cutting-edge engineers, mathematicians, and physicists.

The problem solving and adjusting are what makes the sport so exciting."

—NASCAR fan Gary Krupp, Columbus Air Force Base, Mississippi

In between building the car and servicing it during the race, it is also the job of the crew to push Darrell Waltrip's ride

from the NASCAR inspection area to the starting grid.

"This is a business for me, but it has to be a hobby, too. I had cars running

reality when they crashed. You know it's going to be tough when you come in,

146

The rumble strips along the winding road course at Sears Point Raceway in Sonoma, California, create different problems for NASCAR drivers.

one-two-three recently. There was a five-second high of euphoria followed by

but I don't know if you know **how** tough it's going to be. It's the best thing I've done."

—Felix Sabates, owner of three cars in the NASCAR Winston Cup Series

"After ten years of hard work, close calls, and record-breaking seasons, I can say

that we have been through it all in this relationship. We've worked on it and honed it

to be what it is today . . . a true championship effort."

—Car owner Jack Roush on his association with driver Mark Martin

Standing on a pit wall, Roush looks up the track for one of the three cars he owns in the NASCAR Winston Cup Series.

Mark Martin is among NASCAR's more versatile drivers. Equally at home on a short track, a road course, and a superspeedway, Martin wins regularly in the NASCAR Winston Cup Series and holds the record for all-time wins in the NASCAR Busch Series.

"We had been cheated so much.

The drivers were all after the same thing.

We wanted to get a sanitary racing

organization so that when

we got done racing, we'd get paid."

—Sammy Packard, one of the drivers who attended the

organizational meeting of the National Association for

Stock Car Auto Racing

Bill France's dream of launching a national sanctioning body to

regulate and organize stock car racing came to fruition during

a four-day meeting at the Streamline Hotel in Daytona Beach,

Florida, December 14–17, 1947.

The hauler lineup at any NASCAR Winston Cup event is as bright and shiny as the race cars. In addition to carrying two cars and twenty-five tons of supplies—including driver's lounge. Men like Bostick, who spends his Sunday afternoons as the gas man on a Felix Sabates crew, are in charge of the trailer's inventory and loading. In his

another ten to twelve of us following along. After a race, everyone else gets

the shop and the last ones home." —Team Sabco's Richard Bostick on the life of a NASCAR hauler driver

a 3,000-pound tool chest, two carts, up to one hundred springs, a welder, and enough spare parts to outfit a third car—the front of the fifty-one-foot trailer doubles as the spare time, Bostick is responsible for washing and polishing his rig.

"If we're in no hurry, it takes us two hours to change an engine. But if pressed, we'll do it in forty-five minutes. It's a team thing. Every man has a certain job to do. It runs like clockwork. It's a very precise operation."

—Lowes crew chief Kevin Hamlin

"We shouldn't be seen as part of the show.

The show should be drivers in door-to-door racing.

We work behind the scenes to make the playing field level.

If no one knows we're there, we're happy."

—NASCAR Winston Cup director Gary Nelson

Nelson's team of seventy-five officials handles everything from pre-race and post-race technical inspections, to scoring and rules interpretation, to implementation and compliance. Strict compliance with a comprehensive set of rules is a cornerstone of NASCAR racing. "We are committed to three things," said Nelson, "safety, competition on the track, and keeping the costs down." During a race weekend, members of Nelson's team begin arriving at the track at 6 A.M. and don't depart until after the last garage is closed.

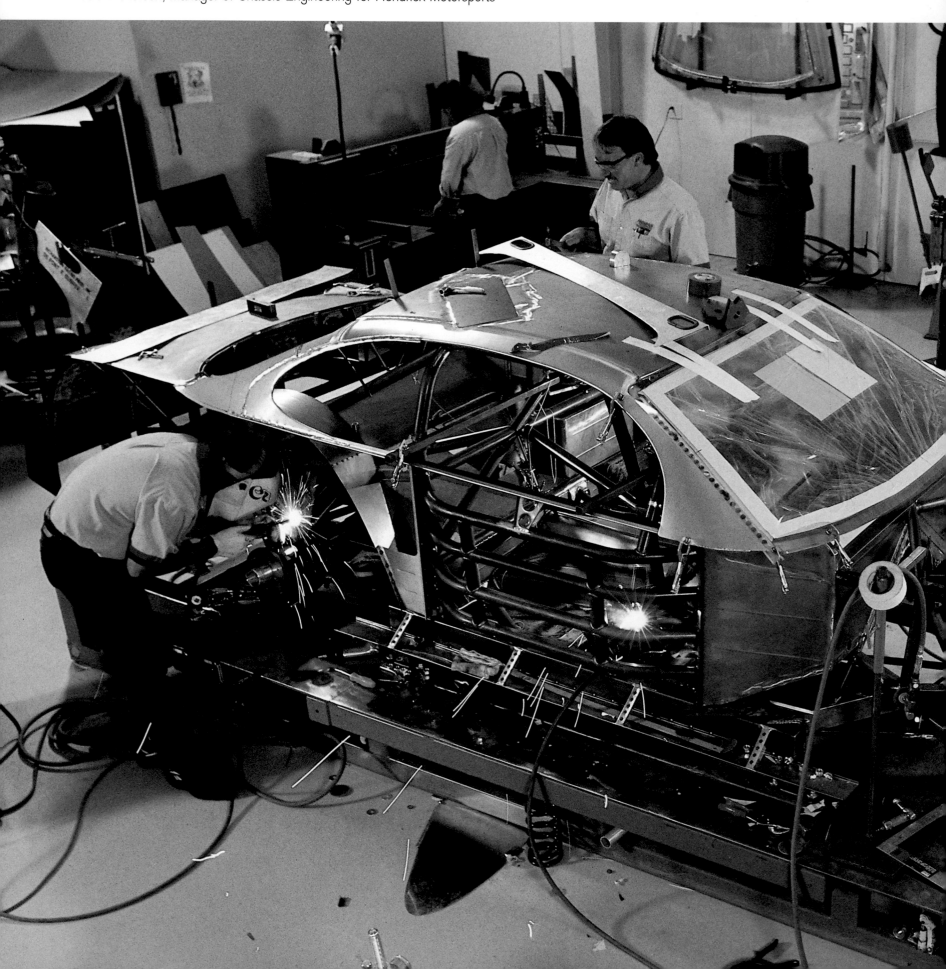

"The season never ends for us. But it must be a great job, because we've got

—Eddie Dickerson, manager of Chassis Engineering for Hendrick Motorsports

some of the finest metal fabricators in the country working in this sport."

The assembly line at Hendrick Chassis **157**
Engineering in Harrisburg, North
Carolina, produces up to thirty NASCAR
Winston Cup cars and NASCAR
Craftsman Trucks a year. Each chassis
takes four to five men a week
to build before it goes to the body shop
for another two hundred hours of finishing work. The car is then shipped to one
of the three Hendrick teams or two other
teams that use Hendrick cars. On
Mondays after races, damaged cars are
returned to Harrisburg for repairs.

"Television opened up NASCAR to the masses. As soon as our races started being televised live, you could feel the change. More media exposure, more fans."

—NASCAR Winston Cup champion driver-turned-commentator Benny Parsons

ABC, CBS, ESPN, TNN, and TBS are all tuned in to NASCAR. The television coverage of NASCAR requires elaborate technical support. Cameras have been fixed to fences, carried by cars, implanted in the surface of several tracks, and mounted on helicopters and blimps circling above. NASCAR has even recorded pit stops from cameras attached to a crewman's hat.

At first glance, they appear to be at opposite ends of the NASCAR spectrum.

Junior Johnson was one of the sport's most successful drivers—then one of its winningest owners.

Junie Donlavey was not a great driver. "My love was about fifty miles an hour faster than my ability." And as an owner, he's won only one race in NASCAR's premier series, although he's been there almost from day one.

Yet, their roles in NASCAR's first half-century are intrinsically linked. "Men like Junior and Junie are at the soul of racing," Ned Jarrett once said during a NASCAR telecast. "They carried the traditions forward."

They do so in their own ways: Johnson with a flare at the front of the pack, Donlavey devotedly somewhat off the pace. But their value to the sport is identical.

"I admire men like Junie," Johnson once said. He's not alone. "Junie was the best owner I've ever known," said Ken Schrader. "He didn't have a lot of resources and backing, but he poured all he had into his car and team."

Johnson won 50 races as a driver plus 140 races and 6 NASCAR Winston Cup Series championships as an owner before retiring. Donlavey has that one race victory in 1981 and has never come close to winning a championship.

But it's how you measure success that's important.

"Money doesn't excite me at all," said Donlavey. "Friends are good. I'd take friends over victories every day. And I've got a lot of friends." Therefore, a lot of victories.

Donlavey gave a number of top drivers their first opportunity. Once they learned the ropes, they moved on to stronger teams. No hard feelings. "I knew what was happening and it never bothered me," said Donlavey. "No one ever left me on bad terms. My former drivers are my friends. The only way I could afford to compete was at a little lower level than the lead pack. But we always put the best car on the track that we could.

"I remember once when Ricky Rudd got out of the car and said, 'Junie, this is the worst car I've even been in.' I told him, 'Son, you're young, you'll forget.'"

Johnson also knew about building fast cars. Before there was NASCAR, he made a living running moonshine on the back roads of North Carolina. "When you grew up in the whiskey business, you got as much excitement as racing," Johnson says. "Either you won or went to prison. Where I grew up, running moonshine wasn't really a bad thing."

Johnson's first NASCAR race was in an altered moonshine car that he drove on the beach at Daytona in 1951. "Speed on the track didn't bother me," Johnson said. "I'd been running faster than that for years on dirt roads between trees."

But he quit driving at age thirty-four to get into the management end of racing.

"They said I was committed to racing," said Johnson. "But I was more involved. It's like a ham-and-egg breakfast. The chicken is involved. The pig is committed."

Junie Donlavey (left) talks shop with longtime friend, Glen Wood (right).

"Seeing those three teams perform

at that level in NASCAR's most prestigious event

against that competition

rivals anything I have ever accomplished."

—Car owner Rick Hendrick

Hendrick (above) lived a car owner's fantasy on February 16, 1997, when his three drivers—Jeff Gordon (center), Terry Labonte (left), and Ricky Craven (right)—finished first, second, and third, respectively, in the Daytona 500.

Among the first successful multicar owners was Carl Kiekhaefer, who also developed the Mercury outboard engine.

With Daytona Beach, Florida, as his backdrop, Kiekhaefer addresses drivers (from left) Charlie Scott, Tim Flock, Fonty Flock, Frank Mundy,

Buck Baker, and Speedy Thompson in front of one of the team's famed Chrysler 300s.

Kiekhaefer won consecutive titles in 1955 and 1956 with Baker and Tim Flock.

Carelli's truck shows that the nose-to-tail racing in the NASCAR Craftsman Truck division is getting closer all the time.

"The damage was pretty minor. A couple whacks with a hammer and

a tug on the left rear panel by the crew and we were back racing."

—NASCAR Craftsman Truck driver Rick Carelli

"Finding excellent pit crew members is almost as tough as finding that championship driver.

Going over the wall is a job that few men can do.

It takes great strength, physical agility, nerves of steel, and absolute attention to detail."

—Bahari Racing crew chief Doug Hewitt

The work is intense, as can be seen by the face of gas catch man Tommy Rigsbee, opposite.

A jackman can raise a 3,400-pound car with two pumps. The men with the air wrenches work in perfect harmony with the tire carrier.

But sometimes, it still takes the nudging of a baseball bat, above, to pound in the fender on Brett Bodine's car.

"Todd and I respect each other's judgments and abilities. We've really improved each other by being honest and committed to the common goal. The search for improvement is never-ending."

—Driver Dale Jarrett on his relationship with crew chief Todd Parrott

For NASCAR crews, the race is only a small part of the equation. Countless hours go into the construction and preparation of the cars and teams, whether it be going over performance charts—as Jarrett and crew chief Todd Parrott do—or climbing backwards through the window and wedging under the dashboard for some last-second adjustments—as a crew member of the Petty Enterprises Pontiac does.

SPIRIT

NASCAR chaplain Max Helton shares a prayer with driver Kenny Irwin Jr. and two members of his crew before a 1997 race at Richmond, Virginia.

Terry Labonte streaks past Old Glory during the Pennsylvania 500 on July 20, 1997, at the Pocono Raceway.

Fifty miles were all that stood between Jack Smith and the checkered flag in the first race of 1960 at Charlotte Motor Speedway.

On a sweltering summer day, in the longest race ever run for stock cars, the competition had fallen by the wayside for a variety of reasons.

Jack Smith had been one of the lucky ones who was still running, and he had lapped every other driver five times or more.

His Sunday drive, though, proved too good to be true. From the first practice session, the racetrack began crumbling and by the final fifty miles of the World 600, the speedway looked like a bombing range, filled with potholes and craters. As Smith was putting yet another lap under his wheels, a chunk of pavement bounced up and gouged a hole in his gas tank.

Smith *screamed* into the pits for repairs, and car owner Bud Moore and his crew went to work. Nothing they tried would stanch the flood of gas pouring out of the car. In desperation, Moore shouted, "Anybody got any Octagon soap?"

Amazingly, somebody produced a bar of another brand, but it wasn't dense enough to plug the leak. Jack Smith didn't win the World 600, but the effort given was typical of the grit, courage, and tenacity on display for all to see throughout NASCAR's first half-century.

"Whatever it takes." That's a creed by which thousands of drivers and crew members have lived over the last fifty years. Diligently pushing forward in the never-ending search for speed. Never giving up the fight until the checkered flag actually falls. Pursuing a dream in spite of all obstacles, whether of geography, finance, race, or gender.

The field pulls away from the start of NASCAR's first Strictly Stock race (now NASCAR Winston Cup Series) at Charlotte, North Carolina, on June 19, 1949.

From NASCAR's very first race, men and women have fearlessly pursued their dreams.

Frank Christian had two cars in the inaugural NASCAR Strictly Stock race, and his wife, Sara, drove one of them to a 14th-place finish. Sara Christian was the first woman to race with NASCAR, but not the last. In the second event sanctioned by NASCAR, on the Beach-Road course at Daytona Beach, Florida, Christian was joined in the field by Ethel Flock Mobley and

Louise Smith. Smith's car flipped while trying to negotiate a tough turn, and spectators helped her right the car so she could continue. Other women who followed the pioneers' path included Ann Chester, former Indy-car racer Janet Guthrie, Robin McCall, Patty Moise, Debbie Lunsford, Diane Teel, and Lisa Jackson. Shawna Robinson sped to the pole position for the 1994 NASCAR Busch Series race at Atlanta. Robinson also became the first woman to win a NASCAR Goody's Dash Series race when she triumphed at Asheville, North Carolina, June 10, 1988.

Some of Indy-car racing's best never judged it beneath them to try NASCAR racing when time allowed. Dan Gurney, A. J. Foyt, and Troy Ruttman finished one-two-three in stock cars at Riverside, California, in 1963. Foyt would go on to win the Firecracker 400 at Daytona in 1964 and 1965, and won the 1972 Daytona 500 by more than a lap. Another Indy-car great, Mario Andretti, beat Foyt to Victory Lane in the Daytona 500 by five years.

Another man bitten hard by the racing bug was country music legend Marty Robbins. Robbins didn't race often and never won, but whenever his touring or recording schedules allowed, he would tow his purple race cars to the track and give his fans something else to cheer about.

Even though NASCAR rules strive to sculpt a level playing field, the spirit of innovation has always had its place. As far back as the days of the Beach-Road course, two-way radio conversation between driver and car owner was in place. Carl Kiekhaefer, whose cars won fifty-two of ninety races in 1955–56, went so far as to hire a meteorologist to accompany his teams and provide up-to-date readings on humidity and other weather data.

A weatherman would have been a welcome addition for most of the early NASCAR teams. Today, teams and fans can get weather information right at the track from NASCAR Online.

Races were held in every corner of the country, from Dog Track Speedway in tiny Moyock, North Carolina, to an airport at Linden, New Jersey, to Chicago's venerable Soldier

Fred Lorenzen was the first driver to earn $100,000 in a season in 1964.

Field, to McCormick Field in Asheville, North Carolina, where Lee Petty crashed into one of the dugouts.

Just as Sara Christian paved the way for women drivers, so did Joie Ray for African American drivers, in 1952. Charlie Scott, Randy Beathea, George Wiltshire, and Willy T. Ribbs all took a shot at NASCAR Winston Cup racing, but only one African

American driver has been able to become a NASCAR fixture—and a winner—among the regulars.

Wendell Scott, a two-time state champion in Virginia, started racing in NASCAR's top division in 1961. With his sons serving as his crew, Scott was able to hold his own as long as his money and stamina held out. Scott raced until 1971 against the Pettys, Pearsons, Yarboroughs, Allisons, and Bakers.

On December 1, 1963, Buck Baker was flagged as the winner of a two-hundred-lap dirt event at Jacksonville (Florida) Speedway Park. Scott, who was age forty-two at the time, protested strongly that he, not Baker, was the rightful winner. "I knew I had won that race," Scott insisted. "I had lapped Buck three times."

Finally, some four hours later, after nearly all five thousand spectators had headed for home, the scorecards proved Scott was right. He had taken the lead from Richard Petty on lap 176, and had actually run 202 laps—two more than needed. Scott was paid the $1,500 first-place prize, but someone else made off with the winner's trophy before Scott saw it. His inspiring life story was later told in "Greased Lightning," a movie with Richard Pryor in the starring role as the hardscrabble mechanic turned driver.

The spirit embodied by Scott was also found in the likes of men such as Walter Ballard and J. D. McDuffie.

McDuffie, like Scott, had mastered the short tracks near home and was willing to live a meager existence for the chance to be a major-league racer. In 1978, McDuffie struck a blow for independent owner-drivers, outhustling Bobby Allison in qualifying to win the pole for the Delaware 500. McDuffie led the first ten laps, but fell victim to a burned piston seventy laps later and finished 33rd. The $1,520 he won was quickly spent—gone to pay for the parts he had charged—but the pride he took in that show of speed dwelled in him.

In 1971, Ballard, a hero of the bullrings near Houston, turned to his wife, Katie, and informed her that he was "going to go run with Richard Petty and those guys for one year." He made good on his vow and, with his preteen sons and

175

Cale Yarborough (car No.27) carried the in-car television camera in the 1982 Daytona 500.

a buddy pitching in as his mechanics, won the '71 Rookie of the Year championship. "I didn't care if I lost everything I owned," Ballard said. "That was my desire in life."

He had plenty of company.

—*Thomas Pope*

"It is what you would expect Roger Penske to build—a great facility. The track is smooth and fast. Everything else is state-of-the-art. Tracks don't get any better than this."

—Mark Martin, winner of four consecutive Winston Cup races in 1993

NASCAR Winston Cup racing returned to Southern California for the first time in nearly a decade on June 22, 1997, with the opening of Roger Penske's new California Speedway in Fontana. The two-mile superspeedway, located an hour's drive east of Los Angeles, drew an overflow crowd for the California 500 inaugural. California Speedway's opening continued NASCAR's move into major population centers.

"One of the few drivers I've seen with the potential to beat a 'Fireball' Roberts

or a Curtis Turner is Dale Earnhardt.

Back then, we had drivers who did it with sheer muscle and will.

Dale is that kind of a driver."

—Former driver and car owner Junior Johnson

Ernie Irvan, opposite, was swarmed for interviews after he returned from serious injuries to win a Daytona 500 qualifying race on February 13, 1996.

In 1994, Dale Earnhardt, above, celebrated his seventh NASCAR Winston Cup Series championship

in New York City's Times Square atop a NASCAR Winston Cup show car.

Sean Monroe

Andy Santerre

Bobby Labonte

Sean Woodside

John Andretti

Elliott Sadler

Bobby Hogge

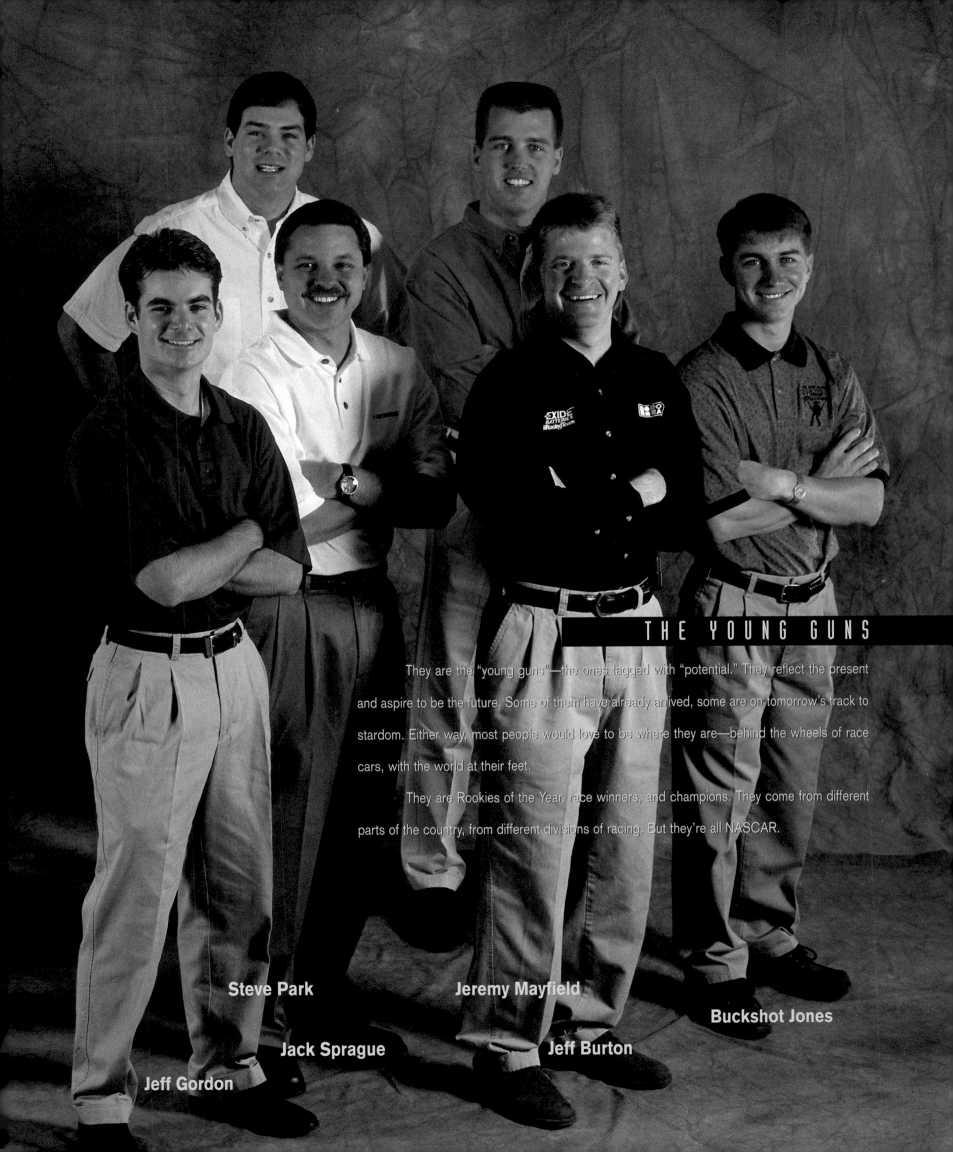

THE YOUNG GUNS

They are the "young guns"—the ones tagged with "potential." They reflect the present and aspire to be the future. Some of them have already arrived, some are on tomorrow's track to stardom. Either way, most people would love to be where they are—behind the wheels of race cars, with the world at their feet.

They are Rookies of the Year, race winners, and champions. They come from different parts of the country, from different divisions of racing. But they're all NASCAR.

Steve Park

Jeremy Mayfield

Buckshot Jones

Jack Sprague

Jeff Burton

Jeff Gordon

"Nobody ever moved over for me on the track.

But no one ever moved over for anyone.

On the track, there were no differences."

—Wendell Scott

On December 1, 1963, in Jacksonville, Florida, Wendell Scott became the first African American to win

a NASCAR Grand National race. A mechanic, Scott drove in the Late Model Sportsman Division

and won the Virginia State Championship in 1959 before joining the NASCAR Grand National tour in 1961.

NASCAR's first superstar, Glenn Roberts, got his nickname "Fireball" not from racing cars but as a star pitcher at the University of Florida. But it fit perfectly into his chosen professional career. Roberts drove everything from modifieds, above, to convertibles to Grand National cars. His thirty-four Grand National wins included the 1959 Firecracker 250, below, at Daytona for Pontiac (car No. 3).

Lance Norick awaits the start of a NASCAR Craftsman Truck race in the Dodge sponsored by the National Hockey League.

For Joe Gibbs, the demands and rewards of owning a NASCAR Winston Cup team offer many of the same challenges he faced as head coach of the Super Bowl champion Washington Redskins.

"Like football, NASCAR racing is very much a team sport," Gibbs said. "There are many parallels.

"I'd say Bobby Labonte is our quarterback as the driver and Jimmy Makar is the coach as the crew chief. Jimmy makes all the decisions at the shop and the racetrack."

That would make Gibbs the general manager.

"My job is to make sure the team has adequate sponsorship to win races and win a championship," said Gibbs.

"I've always said you win with people. I'm a firm believer that cars and parts don't win races, that it's people who make the difference."

Which might explain why competitors from other sports are getting into NASCAR racing.

Former superstars "Dr. J" Julius Erving of the National Basketball Association and Joe Washington of the National Football League have formed a team that will campaign cars in the NASCAR Winston Cup and Busch Series.

Five-time NBA all-star Brad Daugherty has fielded NASCAR Busch cars and NASCAR Craftsman Trucks for Kenny Irwin. The National Hockey League sponsored the NASCAR Craftsman Truck driven by Lance Norick. The Professional Bowlers Association also sponsors a NASCAR Craftsman Truck driven by Terry Cook. And former Redskins quarterback Mark Rypien followed his coach into NASCAR and owned a NASCAR Busch Series car.

"The lure of NASCAR for athletes from other sports is the team aspect of racing," continued Gibbs.

"After their playing careers end, athletes are looking for other ways to keep those competitive fires burning. I was looking for the same thing after football. Racing is a natural. So much goes into making a NASCAR team compete successfully. And, it is exciting."

Veteran crew chief Makar welcomes the athletes from other sports and the fresh ideas they bring to NASCAR.

"Joe has been a wealth of information to me as a leader," said Makar. "Both from his football career and here at the shop, he brings me a lot of knowledge. He's told me on numerous occasions that this is a much harder sport than football simply because there is no off-season."

185

The fourth Brickyard 400 in 1997 drew an estimated 325,000 spectators to the famed two-and-one-half–mile oval.

"Racing at the Indianapolis Motor Speedway that first time in 1994 was probably being at Indy meant—the history and the tradition of the facility. I know it impressed

the biggest thing to happen to the sport during my career. We all knew what the heck out of me." —Darrell Waltrip on racing at the track that previously had hosted only the Indianapolis 500

"I love racing. **That's what drives me.** My father was a driver and I learned from him racing the midgets on the Penske team. The guys back at the shop are the ones who get things together so we can do what we do.

—Rusty Wallace

The fire to win still burns bright in the eyes of 1989 NASCAR Winston Cup Series champion Rusty Wallace.

I have other interests in other things, but racing is what I do. It's that way for all of us on the

Everyone is focused on the car. The day we start thinking 'I' is the day we start having problems."

It's not difficult for Darrell Waltrip to see what NASCAR has meant to him.

"All I have to do is look around every day and count my lucky stars," the veteran driver once said.

"The sport has been good to everyone in it. Which is why I believe we should put something back. And I know my peers feel the same way. Want athletes to be role models? Come see us. We accept the responsibility."

NASCAR is a very benevolent community.

"The generosity of drivers and teams to charitable causes is more easily seen at this level, but it goes on everywhere," said

GIVING BACK

Kyle Petty. "Go to any NASCAR race and I'm sure you'll find someone racing for a cause or raising money for a charity."

Few raise more than Kyle Petty, whose motorcycle charity ride generates $200,000 annually on behalf of three children's hospitals and the NASCAR Winston Cup Racing Wives Auxiliary.

"Kyle is the best spokesman racing will ever have," said car owner Felix Sabates. "He talks with the same sincerity whether it be to his team, a corporate CEO, a man in the street, or a sick child who needs a boost. The man is incredibly loving."

190

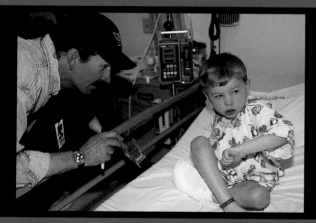 

Left, Kyle Petty takes a break from his charity motorcycle ride to visit a hospitalized child. Darrell Waltrip, center, and Bobby Hamilton, right, host children at the track through their involvement with the Make-A-Wish Foundation.

"I'm no different than a lot of drivers," said Petty.

"There is an attitude in this community that you help out whenever you can," said Rusty Wallace. "Many drivers have received help somewhere along the way. Most of us know what tough times can be like. So we do what we can."

"Almost everyone in the sport is involved in something," said Bill Elliott. "And one driver's cause becomes everyone's cause. Someone wants me to make an appearance for his charity and I try to be there."

"When you get a chance to spend some time with the children at the hospitals,

you get your life into perspective. What we do on the track every week

isn't nearly as important as what those hospitals are doing to help the children."

—Kyle Petty, third-generation NASCAR Winston Cup competitor

A love of motorcycling and a desire to help others led Kyle Petty in 1995 to form the first Kyle Petty's Hot Wheels Charity Tour.

The annual event includes stops at hospitals along the four-day ride, which last year numbered 130 core riders and raised more than $200,000.

"It's not a man-woman deal, it's a racing deal. I don't think the car knows if it's a male or female driving."

—Janet Guthrie, who made thirty-three NASCAR Winston Cup starts between 1976 and 1980 and had five finishes in the top ten

Louise Smith, below, whose NASCAR career began in 1948, is one of ten women to compete in NASCAR Winston Cup racing.

"I don't like the oddity value of being the only woman in a field. I'd like to see ten of us racing. It's possible. It's not a matter of brute force in a race car. Success is based on the ability to withstand heat and maintain concentration. I don't think those are gender-based issues."

—Driver Patty Moise, right, who has made five NASCAR Winston Cup starts and competes in the NASCAR Busch Series

Sara Christian, above, finished fourteenth in NASCAR's first Strictly Stock race in 1949. Later that year she finished fifth in a race at Langhorn, Pennsylvania, the best finish ever by a woman in NASCAR's premier division.

Driver Mike Skinner signs autographs for NASCAR's new Japanese fans.

"Coming to Japan was a great idea. The reception went beyond my expectations. The Japanese are just like American racing fans. Big, powerful cars impress them. To my surprise, a lot of them knew who we were before we ever got onto the track."

195

—Car owner Richard Childress, below, on NASCAR's first appearance at Suzuka, Japan, in 1996

I grew up in NASCAR. And I loved every minute of it—still do. As early as 1955, I was helping to promote NASCAR at the races at Bowman Gray Stadium. At that time I did everything from tacking up promotional posters all over town to pouring sodas and selling snow cones at the concession booths. Some nights I would even jump in the flag stand and give the drivers the green flag. Humble begin-

LOOKING TOWARD TOMORROW ning indeed. But if you look at the history of America's biggest sports, they probably all had humble beginnings just like NASCAR.

It still amazes me that in the early years when my parents were laying the ground work for what is now the world's most popular form of motorsports, the things that they knew were important then still remain as important today. The hard work and time they dedicated to establishing our hallmarks of close competition and the assurance that each event is an enjoyable experience for families is still the cornerstone of everything we do at NASCAR today, fifty years later.

My parents set the standards and I am proud to say that we have carried on those standards. Even as our sport reaches out to new generations, we will remain committed to sustaining our fans, the heart of our sport, and to encouraging the growing support NASCAR has enjoyed throughout the years. Our competitors, the soul of our sport, will continue to compete with the same grit and determination that their predecessors showed during the last five decades. And as NASCAR continues to grow and build, we are certain we will have as much to celebrate and be thankful for in the next fifty years as we have these past fifty.

We know what makes this sport special and what sets NASCAR apart from the rest. Our goals, just as they were when we first began, are to lead NASCAR—our family, our spirit, and the competition—into the second half-century with the same incredible focus and determination, and to deliver to our fans what they have come to expect from NASCAR—the very best in motorsports and entertainment.

—Bill France Jr.

Daytona Beach, Florida

December 1997

SPEEDWAY DIVISION
1952 - Buck Baker, Charlotte, NC
1953 - Pete Allen, Dayton, OH

MIDGET DIVISION
1953 - Nick Fornoro, Danbury, CT
1954 - Chuck Arnold, Stamford, CT
1955 - Fred Meeker, Norwalk, CT (Offy)
      Roger Bailey, Patchogue, NY (Ford)
1956 - Fred Meeker, Norwalk, CT (Offy)
      Johnny Mann, Brooklyn, NY (Ford)
1957 - Jim Whitman, Montclair, NJ (Offy)
      Bob Harkey, Charlotte, NC (Ford)
1958 - Johnny Coy, Freeport, NY
1959 - Jim Whitman, Woodbridge, NJ
1960 - Bernie Wilhelmi, Joliet, IL

LATE MODEL SHORT TRACK DIVISION
1951 - Roscoe Hough, Paterson, NJ
1952 - Neil Cole, Paterson, NJ
1953 - Jim Reed, Peekskill, NY
1954 - Jim Reed, Peekskill, NY
1955 - Jim Reed, Peekskill, NY
1956 - Jim Reed, Peekskill, NY
1957 - Jim Reed, Peekskill, NY
1958 - Lee Petty, Randleman, NC
1959 - Marvin Porter, Lakewood, CA

CONVERTIBLE DIVISION
1955 - Don Oldenberg, Highland, IN
1956 - Bob Welborn, Greensboro, NC
1957 - Bob Welborn, Greensboro, NC
1958 - Bob Welborn, Greensboro, NC
1959 - Joe Lee Johnson, Chattanooga, TN

MODIFIED - SPECIAL DIVISION
1962 - Bobby Allison, Hueytown, AL
1963 - Bobby Allison, Hueytown, AL

GRAND AMERICAN DIVISION
1968 - Tiny Lund, Cross, SC
1969 - Ken Rush, High Point, NC
1970 - Tiny Lund, Cross, SC
1971 - Tiny Lund, Cross, SC
1972 - Wayne Andrews, Siler City, NC

GRAND NATIONAL EAST DIVISION
1972 - Neil Castles, Charlotte, NC
1973 - Tiny Lund, Cross, SC

GRAND AMERICAN STOCK CAR DIVISION
1980 - Junior Niedecken, Pensacola, FL
1981 - Junior Niedecken, Pensacola, FL
1982 - Jerry Lawley, Cantonment, FL
1983 - Mike Alexander, Franklin, TN

NASCAR WINSTON ALL-AMERICAN CHALLENGE SERIES
1984 - Mike Alexander, Franklin, TN
1985 - Dave Mader III, Maylene, AL
1986 - Dave Mader III, Maylene, AL
1987 - Dave Mader III, Maylene, AL
1988 - Dave Mader III, Maylene, AL
1989 - Stanley Smith, Chelsea, AL
1990 - Mike Garvey, Muskegon, MI

NASCAR SLIM JIM ALL PRO SERIES
1991 - Jody Ridley, Chatsworth, GA
1992 - Jody Ridley, Chatsworth, GA
1993 - Jody Ridley, Chatsworth, GA
1994 - Mike Cope, Pinellas Park, FL
1995 - Hal Goodson, Darlington, SC
1996 - Mike Cope, Pinellas Park, FL
1997   Hal Goodson, Darlington, SC

NASCAR GOODY'S DASH SERIES
1975 - Dean Combs, North Wilkesboro, NC
1976 - Dean Combs, North Wilkesboro, NC
1977 - Dean Combs, North Wilkesboro, NC
1978 - Larry Hoopaugh, Charlotte, NC
1979 - Larry Hoopaugh, Charlotte, NC
1980 - Dean Combs, North Wilkesboro, NC
1981 - Dean Combs, North Wilkesboro, NC
1982 - Larry Hoopaugh, Charlotte, NC
1983 - Michael Waltrip, Owensboro, KY
1984 - Mike Swaim, High Point, NC
1985 - Mike Swaim, High Point, NC
1986 - Hut Stricklin, Calera, AL
1987 - Larry Caudill, North Wilkesboro, NC
1988 - Larry Caudill, North Wilkesboro, NC
1989 - Gary Wade Finley, Huntsville, AL
1990 - Robert Huffman, Claremont, NC
1991 - Johnny Chapman, Stony Point, NC
1992 - Mickey York, Asheboro, NC
1993 - Rodney Orr, Palm Coast, FL
1994 - Will Hobgood, Winnsboro, SC
1995 - David Hutto, Rock Hill, SC
1996 - Lyndon Amick, Batesburg, SC
1997 - Mike Swaim Jr., High Point, NC

NASCAR NORTH TOUR
1979 - Beaver Dragon, Milton, VT
1980 - Beaver Dragon, Milton, VT
1981 - Dick McCabe, Kennebunkport, ME
1982 - Dick McCabe, Kennebunkport, ME
1983 - Robbie Crouch, Tampa, FL
1984 - Robbie Crouch, Tampa, FL
1985 - Randy LaJoie, Norwalk, CT

NASCAR BUSCH ALL-STAR SUPER SERIES
1984 - Jerry Inmon, Bruce, MS
1985 - Ronnie Johnson, Chattanooga, TN
1986 - Jeff Purvis, Clarksville, TN

NASCAR REB-CO NORTHWEST TOUR
1985 - Garrett Evans, Ardenvoir, WA
1986 - Ron Eaton, Tacoma, WA
1987 - Tobey Butler, Kirkland, WA
1988 - Ron Eaton, Tacoma, WA
1989 - Garrett Evans, Ardenvoir, WA
1990 - John Dillon, Boise, ID
1991 - Monte English, Port Angeles, WA
1992 - Dirk Stephens, Tumwater, WA
1993 - Kirk Rogers, Spokane, WA
1994 - Garrett Evans, Ardenvoir, WA
1995 - Ron Eaton, Tacoma, WA
1996 - Kelly Tanner, Woodinville, WA
1997 - Kelly Tanner, Woodinville, WA

NASCAR FEATHERLITE SOUTHWEST TOUR
1986 - Ron Esau, Lakeside, CA
1987 - Mike Chase, Bakersfield, CA
1988 - Roman Calczynski, Sepulveda, CA
1989 - Dan Press, Frazier Park, CA
1990 - Doug George, Atwater, CA
1991 - Rick Carelli, Arvada, CO
1992 - Ron Hornaday Jr., Palmdale, CA
1993 - Ron Hornaday Jr., Palmdale, CA
1994 - Steve Portenga, Reno, NV
1995 - Lance Hooper, Palmdale, CA
1996 - Chris Raudman, Redding, CA
1997 - Bryan Germone, Windsor, CA

NASCAR BUSCH ALL-STAR TOUR
1985 - Roger Dolan, Lisbon, IA
1986 - Joe Kosiski, Omaha, NE
1987 - Steve Kosiski, Omaha, NE
1988 - Joe Kosiski, Omaha, NE
1989 - Joe Kosiski, Omaha, NE
1990 - Steve Kosiski, Omaha, NE
1991 - Steve Kosiski, Omaha, NE
1992 - Steve Kosiski, Omaha, NE
1993 - Bob Hill, Story City, IA
1994 - Steve Kosiski, Omaha, NE
1995 - Steve Kosiski, Omaha, NE
1996 - Joe Kosiski, Omaha, NE
1997 - Joe Kosiski, Omaha, NE

NASCAR BUSCH NORTH SERIES, GRAND NATIONAL DIVISION
1987 - Joey Kourafas, Randolph, MA
1988 - Jamie Aube, North Ferrisburg, VT
1989 - Jamie Aube, North Ferrisburg, VT
1990 - Jamie Aube, North Ferrisburg, VT
1991 - Ricky Craven, Newburgh, ME
1992 - Dick McCabe, Kennebunkport, ME
1993 - Dick McCabe, Kennebunkport, ME
1994 - Dale Shaw, Center Conway, NH
1995 - Kelly Moore, Scarborough, ME
1996 - Dave Dion, Hudson, NH
1997 - Mike Stefanik, Coventry, RI

NASCAR MODIFIED DIVISION
1948 - Red Byron, Atlanta, GA
1949 - Fonty Flock, Atlanta, GA
1950 - Charles Dyer, North Bergen, NJ
1951 - Wally Campbell, Trenton, NJ
1952 - Frankie Schneider, Sandbrook, NJ
1953 - Joe Weatherly, Norfolk, VA
1954 - Jack Choquette, West Palm Beach, FL
1955 - Bill Widenhouse, Midland, NC
1956 - Red Farmer, Hialeah, FL
1957 - Ken Marriott, Palm Harbor, FL
1958 - Budd Olsen, Paulsboro, NJ
1959 - Glenn Guthrie, Washington, DC
1960 - Johnny Roberts, Baltimore, MD
1961 - Johnny Roberts, Baltimore, MD
1962 - Eddie Crouse, Glen Allen, VA
1963 - Eddie Crouse, Glen Allen, VA
1964 - Bobby Allison, Hueytown, AL
1965 - Bobby Allison, Hueytown, AL
1966 - Ernie Gahan, Dover, NH
1967 - Bugs Stevens, Rehoboth, MA
1968 - Bugs Stevens, Rehoboth, MA
1969 - Bugs Stevens, Rehoboth, MA
1970 - Fred DeSarro, Hope Valley, RI
1971 - Jerry Cook, Rome, NY
1972 - Jerry Cook, Rome, NY
1973 - Richie Evans, Rome, NY
1974 - Jerry Cook, Rome, NY
1975 - Jerry Cook, Rome, NY
1976 - Jerry Cook, Rome, NY
1977 - Jerry Cook, Rome, NY
1978 - Richie Evans, Rome, NY
1979 - Richie Evans, Rome, NY
1980 - Richie Evans, Rome, NY
1981 - Richie Evans, Rome, NY
1982 - Richie Evans, Rome, NY
1983 - Richie Evans, Rome, NY
1984 - Richie Evans, Rome, NY

NASCAR FEATHERLITE MODIFIED TOUR
1985 - Richie Evans, Rome, NY
1986 - Jimmy Spencer, Berwick, PA

1987 - Jimmy Spencer, Berwick, PA
1988 - Mike McLaughlin, Waterloo, NY
1989 - Mike Stefanik, Coventry, RI
1990 - Jamie Tomaino, Howell, NJ
1991 - Mike Stefanik, Coventry, RI
1992 - Jeff Fuller, Auburn, MA
1993 - Rick Fuller, Auburn, MA
1994 - Wayne Anderson, Yaphank, NY
1995 - Tony Hirschman, Northampton, PA
1996 - Tony Hirschman, Northampton, PA
1997 - Mike Stefanik, Coventry, RI

NASCAR WINSTON WEST SERIES

1954 - Lloyd Dane, Lakewood, CA
1955 - Danny Letner, Downey, CA
1956 - Lloyd Dane, Lakewood, CA
1957 - Lloyd Dane, Lakewood, CA
1958 - Eddie Gray, Gardena, CA
1959 - Bob Ross, Lakewood, CA
1960 - Marvin Porter, Lakewood, CA
1961 - Eddie Gray, Gardena, CA
1962 - Eddie Gray, Gardena, CA
1963 - Ron Hornaday, San Fernando, CA
1964 - Ron Hornaday, San Fernando, CA
1965 - Bill Amick, Portland, OR
1966 - Jack McCoy, Modesto, CA
1967 - Scotty Cain, Fresno, CA
1968 - Scotty Cain, Fresno, CA
1969 - Ray Elder, Caruthers, CA
1970 - Ray Elder, Caruthers, CA
1971 - Ray Elder, Caruthers, CA
1972 - Ray Elder, Caruthers, CA
1973 - Jack McCoy, Modesto, CA
1974 - Ray Elder, Caruthers, CA
1975 - Ray Elder, Caruthers, CA
1976 - Chuck Bown, Portland, OR
1977 - Bill Schmitt, Redding, CA
1978 - Jim Insolo, Mission Hills, CA
1979 - Bill Schmitt, Redding, CA
1980 - Roy Smith, Victoria, BC, Canada
1981 - Roy Smith, Victoria, BC, Canada
1982 - Roy Smith, Victoria, BC, Canada
1983 - Jim Robinson, North Hollywood, CA
1984 - Jim Robinson, North Hollywood, CA
1985 - Jim Robinson, North Hollywood, CA
1986 - Hershel McGriff, Bridal Veil, OR
1987 - Chad Little, Spokane, WA
1988 - Roy Smith, Victoria, BC, Canada
1989 - Bill Schmitt, Redding, CA
1990 - Bill Schmitt, Redding, CA
1991 - Bill Sedgwick, Aga Dulce, CA
1992 - Bill Sedgwick, Aga Dulce, CA
1993 - Rick Carelli, Arvada, CO
1994 - Mike Chase, Bakersfield, CA
1995 - Doug George, Atwater, CA
1996 - Lance Hooper, Palmdale, CA
1997 - Butch Gilliland, Anaheim, CA

NASCAR WINSTON RACING SERIES NATIONAL CHAMPION

1982 - Tom Hearst, Muscatine, IA
1983 - Mike Alexander, Franklin, TN
1984 - David Into, Hardeeville, SC
1985 - Doug McCoun, Prunedale, CA
1986 - Joe Kosiski, Omaha, NE
1987 - Roger Dolan, Lisbon, IA
1988 - Robert Powell, Moncks Corner, SC
1989 - Larry Phillips, Springfield, MO
1990 - Max Prestwood, Lenoir, NC
1991 - Larry Phillips, Springfield, MO
1992 - Larry Phillips, Springfield, MO
1993 - Barry Beggarly, Pelham, NC
1994 - David Rogers, Orlando, FL
1995 - Larry Phillips, Springfield, MO
1996 - Larry Phillips, Springfield, MO
1997 - Dexter Canipe, Clermont, NC

NASCAR WINSTON RACING SERIES CENTRAL REGION

1982 - Tom Hearst, Muscatine, IA
1983 - Roger Dolan, Lisbon, IA
1984 - Ken Walton, Viola, IA
1985 - Steve Kosiski, Omaha, NE
1986 - Joe Kosiski, Omaha, NE
1987 - Roger Dolan, Lisbon, IA
1988 - Dale Fischlein, Davenport, IA
1989 - Ray Guss Jr., Milan, IL
1990 - Ray Guss Jr., Milan, IL
1991 - Ray Guss Jr., Milan, IL
1992 - Joe Kosiski, Omaha, NE
1993 - Steve Boley, Oxford, IA
1994 - Mark Burgtorf, Quincy, IL
1995 - Ray Guss Jr., Milan, IL

NASCAR WINSTON RACING SERIES EASTERN SEABOARD REGION

1989 - Jimmy Hatchell, Florence, SC
1990 - Dave Pletcher, Clearwater, FL
1991 - Sean Graham, Moncks Corner, SC
1992 - Mike Love, Pendergrass, GA
1993 - Jerry Williams, Summerville, SC
1994 - David Rogers, Orlando, FL
1995 - Jon Compagnone Jr., Orange City, FL

NASCAR WINSTON RACING SERIES SOUTHEAST REGION

1982 - Ronnie Sanders, Fayetteville, GA
1983 - Mike Alexander, Franklin, TN
1984 - David Into, Hardeeville, SC
1985 - Charles Powell III, Moncks Corner, SC
1986 - Robert Powell, Moncks Corner, SC
1987 - Mike Love, Pendergrass, GA
1988 - Robert Powell, Moncks Corner, SC

NASCAR WINSTON RACING SERIES GREAT NORTHERN REGION

1989 - Kevin Nuttleman, Bangor, WI
1990 - Jeff Hinkemeyer, St. Cloud, MN
1991 - Eddy McKean, Jerome, ID
1992 - Steve Murgic, Rosemount, MN
1993 - Mel Walen, Shakopee, MN
1994 - John Knaus, Rockford, IL
1995 - Mel Walen, Shakopee, MN

NASCAR WINSTON RACING SERIES MID-AMERICA REGION

1989 - Larry Phillips, Springfield, MO
1990 - Mike Wallace, St. Louis, MO
1991 - Larry Phillips, Springfield, MO
1992 - Larry Phillips, Springfield, MO
1993 - Larry Phillips, Springfield, MO
1994 - Dale Planck, Homer, NY
1995 - Dale Planck, Homer, NY
1996 - Mike VanSparrentak, Kalamazoo, MI
1997 - Paul Proksch, Stoddard, WI

NASCAR WINSTON RACING SERIES MID-ATLANTIC REGION

1932 - Sam Ard, Asheboro, NC
1933 - Sam Ard, Asheboro, NC
1934 - Elton Sawyer, Chesapeake, VA
1935 - Elton Sawyer, Chesapeake, VA
1936 - Bubba Adams, Chesapeake, VA
1937 - Robert Pressley, Asheville, NC
1938 - Robert Pressley, Asheville, NC
1989 - Bob Pressley, Asheville, NC
1990 - Max Prestwood, Lenoir, NC
1991 - Johnny Rumley, Winston-Salem, NC
1992 - Michael Ritch, High Point, NC
1993 - Barry Beggarly, Pelham, NC
1994 - Barry Beggarly, Pelham, NC
1995 - Phil Warren, Norfolk, VA

NASCAR WINSTON RACING SERIES NORTHEAST REGION

1982 - Richie Evans, Rome, NY
1983 - Richie Evans, Rome, NY
1984 - Richie Evans, Rome, NY
1985 - Richie Evans, Rome, NY
1986 - George Kent, Horseheads, NY
1987 - Steve Peles, Glen Campbell, PA
1988 - Glenn Gault, Hubbard, OH
1989 - Jan Leaty, Williamson, NY
1990 - Steve Peles, Glen Campbell, PA
1991 - Jerry Marquis, Enfield, CT
1992 - Charlie Cragan, Hopewell, PA
1993 - Charlie Cragan, Hopewell, PA
1994 - Charlie Cragan, Hopewell, PA
1995 - Jeff Wildung, Nassau, MN
1996 - John Blewett III, Howell, NJ
1997 - Jeffrey Dunmyer, Friedens, PA

NASCAR WINSTON RACING SERIES PACIFIC COAST REGION

1982 - Doug Williams, Merced, CA
1983 - Dave Byrd, Los Gatos, CA
1984 - Jim Pettit II, Seaside, CA
1985 - Doug McCoun, Prunedale, CA
1986 - Doug McCoun, Prunedale, CA
1987 - Bob Fox, Bremerton, WA
1988 - Ed Sans Jr., Santa Clara, CA
1989 - Bobby Hogge, Salinas, CA
1990 - Jeff Silva, Aptos, CA
1991 - Ron Bradley, Pasco, WA
1992 - Steve Hendren, Santa Cruz, CA
1993 - Robert Miller, San Jose, CA
1994 - Larry Phillips, Springfield, MO
1995 - Larry Phillips, Springfield, MO
1996 - Bobby Hogge IV, Salinas, CA
1997 - Bobby Hogge IV, Salinas, CA

NASCAR WINSTON RACING SERIES SUNBELT REGION

1987 - Carl Trimmer, Tucson, AZ
1988 - James Cline, Anniston, AL
1989 - Paul White, Temple, TX
1990 - Bo Rawdon, Mansfield, TX
1991 - David Rogers, Orlando, FL
1992 - Ricky Icenhower, Fairgrove, MO
1993 - Tony Ponder, Deland, FL
1994 - Paul Peeples, McKinleyville, CA
1995 - Paul White, Temple, TX
1996 - Carl Trimmer, Tucson, AZ
1997 - Keith Green, Robinson, TX

NASCAR WINSTON RACING SERIES HEARTLAND REGION

1996 - Larry Phillips, Springfield, MO
1997 - Andy Kirby, Whitehouse, TN

NASCAR WINSTON RACING SERIES ATLANTIC SEABOARD REGION

1996 - Wes Troup, Riverdale, MD
1997 - Allen Chillers Jr., Summerville, SC

NASCAR WINSTON RACING SERIES BLUE RIDGE REGION

1996 - Steven Howard, Greer, SC
1997 - Dexter Canipe, Clermont NC

NASCAR WINSTON RACING SERIES MIDWEST REGION

1996 - Steve Boley, Oxford, IA
1997 - Jeffrey Martin, Webster, MN

NASCAR WINSTON RACING SERIES GREAT WEST REGION

1996 - Eddy McKean, Jerome, ID
1997 - Bruce Yackey, Greely, CO

NASCAR WINSTON RACING SERIES
NEW ENGLAND REGION
1996 - Dale Planck, Homer, NY
1997 - Jimmy Broderick, Brookfield, CT

NASCAR WINSTON CUP SERIES
1949 - Red Byron, Atlanta, GA
1950 - Bill Rexford, Conewango Valley, NY
1951 - Herb Thomas, Sanford, NC
1952 - Tim Flock, Atlanta, GA
1953 - Herb Thomas, Sanford, NC
1954 - Lee Petty, Randleman, NC
1955 - Tim Flock, Atlanta, GA
1956 - Buck Baker, Charlotte, NC
1957 - Buck Baker, Charlotte, NC
1958 - Lee Petty, Randleman, NC
1959 - Lee Petty, Randleman, NC
1960 - Rex White, Spartanburg, SC
1961 - Ned Jarrett, Conover, NC
1962 - Joe Weatherly, Norfolk, VA
1963 - Joe Weatherly, Norfolk, VA
1964 - Richard Petty, Randleman, NC
1965 - Ned Jarrett, Camden, SC
1966 - David Pearson, Spartanburg, SC
1967 - Richard Petty, Randleman, NC
1968 - David Pearson, Spartanburg, SC
1969 - David Pearson, Spartanburg, SC
1970 - Bobby Isaac, Catawba, NC
1971 - Richard Petty, Randleman, NC

1972 - Richard Petty, Randleman, NC
1973 - Benny Parsons, Ellerbe, NC
1974 - Richard Petty, Randleman, NC
1975 - Richard Petty, Randleman, NC
1976 - Cale Yarborough, Timmonsville, SC
1977 - Cale Yarborough, Timmonsville, SC
1978 - Cale Yarborough, Timmonsville, SC
1979 - Richard Petty, Randleman, NC
1980 - Dale Earnhardt, Kannapolis, NC
1981 - Darrell Waltrip, Franklin, TN
1982 - Darrell Waltrip, Franklin, TN
1983 - Bobby Allison, Hueytown, AL
1984 - Terry Labonte, Corpus Christi, TX
1985 - Darrell Waltrip, Franklin, TN
1986 - Dale Earnhardt, Kannapolis, NC
1987 - Dale Earnhardt, Kannapolis, NC
1988 - Bill Elliott, Dawsonville, GA
1989 - Rusty Wallace, St. Louis, MO
1990 - Dale Earnhardt, Kannapolis, NC
1991 - Dale Earnhardt, Kannapolis, NC
1992 - Alan Kulwicki, Greenfield, WI
1993 - Dale Earnhardt, Kannapolis, NC
1994 - Dale Earnhardt, Kannapolis, NC
1995 - Jeff Gordon, Pittsboro, IN
1996 - Terry Labonte, Corpus Christi, TX
1997 - Jeff Gordon, Pittsboro, IN

NASCAR CRAFTSMAN TRUCK SERIES
1995 - Mike Skinner, Susanville, CA

1996 - Ron Hornaday Jr., Palmdale, CA
1997 - Jack Sprague, Spring Lake, MI

NASCAR LATE MODEL
SPORTSMAN DIVISION
1950 - Mike Klapak, Warren, OH
1951 - Mike Klapak, Warren, OH
1952 - Mike Klapak, Warren, OH
1953 - Johnny Roberts, Baltimore, MD
1954 - Danny Graves, Gardena, CA
1955 - Billy Myers, Germanton, NC
1956 - Ralph Earnhardt, Kannapolis, NC
1957 - Ned Jarrett, Conover, NC
1958 - Ned Jarrett, Conover, NC
1959 - Rick Henderson, Petaluma, CA
1960 - Bill Wimble, Lisbon, NY
1961 - Dick Nephew, Mooers Forks, NY
         Bill Wimble, Lisbon, NY (co-champions)
1962 - Rene Charland, Agawam, MA
1963 - Rene Charland, Agawam, MA
1964 - Rene Charland, Agawam, MA
1965 - Rene Charland, Agawam, MA
1966 - Don MacTavish, Dover, MA
1967 - Pete Hamilton, Dedham, MA
1968 - Joe Thurman, Rocky Mount, VA
1969 - Red Farmer, Hueytown, AL
1970 - Red Farmer, Hueytown, AL
1971 - Red Farmer, Hueytown, AL
1972 - Jack Ingram, Asheville, NC

1973 - Jack Ingram, Asheville, NC
1974 - Jack Ingram, Asheville, NC
1975 - L. D. Ottinger, Newport, TN
1976 - L. D. Ottinger, Newport, TN
1977 - Butch Lindley, Greenville, SC
1978 - Butch Lindley, Greenville, SC
1979 - Gene Glover, Kingsport, TN
1980 - Morgan Shepherd, Conover, NC
1981 - Tommy Ellis, Richmond, VA

NASCAR BUSCH SERIES,
GRAND NATIONAL DIVISION
1982 - Jack Ingram, Asheville, NC
1983 - Sam Ard, Asheboro, NC
1984 - Sam Ard, Asheboro, NC
1985 - Jack Ingram, Asheville, NC
1986 - Larry Pearson, Spartanburg, SC
1987 - Larry Pearson, Spartanburg, SC
1988 - Tommy Ellis, Richmond, VA
1989 - Rob Moroso, Madison, CT
1990 - Chuck Bown, Portland, OR
1991 - Bobby Labonte, Corpus Christi, TX
1992 - Joe Nemechek, Lakeland, FL
1993 - Steve Grissom, Gadsden, AL
1994 - David Green, Owensboro, KY
1995 - Johnny Benson, Grand Rapids, MI
1996 - Randy LaJoie, Norwalk, CT
1997 - Randy LaJoie, Norwalk, CT

200

CREDITS

AUTHOR/EDITOR

BILL CENTER, author/editor, has covered NASCAR for the past twenty years. A distinguished writer for The San Diego Union-Tribune since 1967, Bill writes feature stories on motor racing, boxing, baseball, and basketball and has received many awards, including state-wide journalism awards for his coverage of the 1983 America's Cup. Bill is a 47-year resident of San Diego, California.

CONTRIBUTING AUTHORS

Monte Dutton is with the Gaston Gazette in Gastonia, North Carolina.
Mike Hembree is with the Greenville News in South Carolina.
Tom Higgins is a freelance writer based in Mooresville, North Carolina.
Richard Huff is with the New York Daily News.
Hunter James is a freelance writer based in South Carolina.

Bob Moore is a freelance writer based in Lexington, North Carolina.
Gerald Martin is with the Raleigh News & Observer in Raliegh, North Carolina.
Thomas Pope is with the Fayetteville Observer.
Steve Waid is editor of Winston Cup Scene.

CONTRIBUTING PHOTOGRAPHERS

Andres R. Alonso: 27f, 28a-d, j-k, 46a, 46-47, 58, 94, 120, 124c, 137, 143a,c, 145, 148, 149, 154, 155, 158a, 160, 164-165, 166, 170-171, 184.
Bowman Gray Stadium: 63b.
Phil Cavali/NASCAR Winston Cup Scene: 14-15, 32a, 32-33, 44-45, 50a, 54, 68-69, 104 105, 114a,118, 121, 138a, 159b, 162b, 167.
The Daytona Beach News-Journal: 108-109.
Daytona Racing Archives: 8-9, 21, 25a-j, 26a-q, 27a-e,g-l, 48 a-d, 50 b-c, 51 a-c, 55, 59, 62, 71, 73a, 78-79, 80, 83, 86-87, 87 a-f, 102, 103 a-b, 110, 112a, 125, 131, 132a-b,

133, 144a,c, 150-151, 151b, 161, 163, 173, 174a-b, 175a-b, 182, 183a-b, 192-193, 193c.
Darrel Dennis: 135.
Butch Dill: 116-117, 142, 143b.
Chad Fletcher/NASCAR Winston Cup Scene: 42, 52-53.
Jim Fluharty/NASCAR Winston Cup Illustrated: 5, 124a, 191.
Ladon George/NASCAR Winston Cup Illustrated: 12-13, 16-17, 56-57, 114-115, 190a.
Greenville Pickens: 63a.
Hierwarter Photography: 43b.

International Speedway Corporation: 2-3, 24-25, 92-93, 98, 106b-c, 190b-c.
Craig Jones/Allsport: 64-65, 140-141.
Elmer Kappell/NASCAR Winston Cup Illustrated: 70.
Don Kelly/NASCAR Winston Cup Scene: 60b.
Andy Lewis: 197.
Nate Mecca: 43a.
Dozier Mobley: 73c.
Sam Sharpe/NASCAR Winston Cup Illustrated: 178.
Allen Steel/Allsport: 68a.

David Taylor/Allsport: 39, 111, 123b, 188-189.
George Tiedemann: 6-7, 10-11, 18-19, 22-23, 28e-i, 34-35, 36-37, 41, 60a, 61, 66-67, 73b, 76-77, 81, 82, 84-85, 88-89, 90-91, 92a, 96, 97, 99a-c, 100-101, 106a, 106-107, 108a, 112b, 113, 122-123, 126-127, 129, 138-139, 144b, 146-147, 152-153, 156-157, 158 b-c, 159a, c, 162a, 168, 169, 172, 176-177, 179, 186-187, 193b, 194-195, 195b.
Kevin Vandivier: 74-75, 128, 130, 180-181.
Tim Wilcox/NASCAR Winston Cup Illustrated: 44a, 124b.